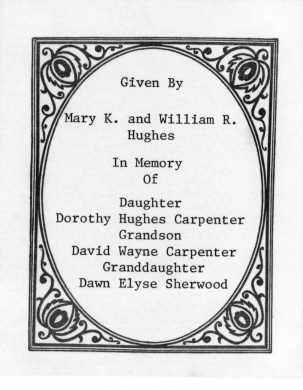

Given By

Mary K. and William R.
Hughes

In Memory
Of

Daughter
Dorothy Hughes Carpenter
Grandson
David Wayne Carpenter
Granddaughter
Dawn Elyse Sherwood

THE ENGLISH FREE CHURCHES

The
English Free Churches

HORTON DAVIES
M.A., D.D., D.Phil.

Henry W. Putnam Professor
of Religion in Princeton University

Second Edition

GREENWOOD PRESS, PUBLISHERS
WESTPORT, CONNECTICUT

Library of Congress Cataloging in Publication Data

Davies, Horton.
    The English free churches.

    Reprint. Originally published: London ; New York :
Oxford University Press, 1963. (Home university library
of modern knowledge ; 220)
        Bibliography: p.
        Includes index.
        1. Free churches--England. 2. England--Church
history. I. Title. II. Series: Home university
library of modern knowledge ; 220.
BR743.2.D38 1985   280'.4   85-7684
ISBN 0-313-20838-7 (lib. bdg. : alk. paper)

This reprint has been authorized by the Oxford University Press

Reprinted in 1985 by Greenwood Press
A division of Congressional Information Service, Inc.
88 Post Road West, Westport, Connecticut 06881

Printed in the United States of America

10 9 8 7 6 5 4 3 2 1

CONTENTS

INTRODUCTION

Two modest claims may perhaps be made for this brief history of the Baptists, Congregationalists, Methodists, and Presbyterians of England known collectively as 'The English Free Churches'. The first is that the ecumenical age in which we live demands that the responsible church historian write in an empathetic, not a polemical, spirit. Denominational trumpets should be muted in the symphony of Church unity. The history of the English Free Churches presupposes, of course, a continuing dialogue with the Church of England from which they dissented and dissent. None the less, it should be conducted with charity. In 1962 Free Churchmen and Anglicans for the most part see each other as allies; in 1662 they saw themselves as inveterate enemies. It is in the newer and more irenic spirit that I have tried to write, setting nothing down in malice.

In the second place, I have tried to indicate the many positive contributions which the English Free Churches at home and abroad have made to the lives of the English-speaking nations. In personal religion understood as a covenant relationship, in their concern to create a theocracy in which the writ of God runs through the social and economic realm, in their experiments in worship and in the Christian life, in their passionate concern for a Christian humanism in education and social welfare, in their laboratories of democracy (the Independent church meetings and Methodist classes), as in their advocacy of modern missions and Christian unity, the English Free Churches have contributed largely to fashioning those spiritual links and values that bind the English-speaking nations. It is significant that those religious communities born in England: Anglicanism, Congregationalism, Methodism, and Quakerism, have produced a rich fruitage in the New World. The Baptists, like the Presbyterians, came to Britain by way of Europe and both have left an indelible impress in English-speaking lands. To read the history of the English Free Churches is, in part, to understand the roots of the transatlantic *entente cordiale*.

H. D.

1962

CHAPTER I

PURITANS AND PREDECESSORS

THE 'English Free Churches' became generally known under that description only after 1896, when the separate non-episcopal communions of England were affiliated to form a National Free Church Council,[1] which included the Congregationalists, Presbyterians, Baptists, and Methodists,[2] with the Society of Friends in sympathy on the periphery of the organization. The affinity of these separate denominations had long been recognized, however, if not by themselves, at least by their opponents under the generic terms of 'Nonconformists' or 'Dissenters', by which negative terms they had been described for the previous two centuries, whilst during the first century of the existence of the English Baptists, Congregationalists, and Presbyterians, they were nicknamed the 'Puritans'.

Into the ancestry of Puritanism this is not the place to enter. Puritanism proper was the outlook of the radical Protestant party in Elizabethan days, who regarded the 'Elizabethan Settlement' as incomplete, a mere half-way house between Rome and Geneva. Their overriding aim was to model English liturgy, discipline, and government according to the 'pure'

[1] In 1940 the Free Church Federal Council was formed in England by a merger of the Federal Council of the Evangelical Free Churches (1919) and the National Council of the Evangelical Free Churches (1896). Cf. H. P. van Dusen, *World Christianity*, p. 277. The first Free Church Congress was held in 1892.

[2] Methodism, of course, appeared on the English scene a century and a half after the other three Dissenting Churches.

Word of God. The name of 'Puritan' was therefore
deserved; nevertheless, the opprobrious epithet stigmatized the party as heretics, bringing to mind the
anathematized medieval *Cathari*. In addition, amongst
the common people the terms 'Puritans' and 'Pre-
cisians' were interchangeable. By the people the Puritan, on account of the strictness and seriousness of his
religion, was regarded as a kill-joy. Indeed, as such, he
has been grossly maligned by the Elizabethan drama-
tists, appearing in the roles of the self-important
Malvolio of Shakespeare, or the interfering, hypocritical
Zeal-of-the-Land-Busy of Ben Jonson. The legacy of
the portrait of the Puritan as a gloomy fanatic, pedantic
and punctilious, censorious and crabbed, has come
down to our own time. It is curiously forgotten that the
Puritans numbered amongst their loyal followers the
gentle Edmund Spenser and the indomitable Walter
Ralegh, the Protector Cromwell and the poet Milton,
in whom religion and refinement, Christianity and
courtesy, were commingled. Their sympathizers, in the
early days, included several bishops, and even the Archbishop of Canterbury, Edmund Grindal, apostrophized
by Spenser in *The Shepheards Calender*. The unforgiv-
able error of these men was that they took religion
seriously, and desired a further Reformation according
to the Word of God.

The impetus to further Reformation on a Biblical
foundation came from Geneva, whence a number of
influential English divines returned to England after
their exile during the Marian persecutions of Protestants. These included William Whittingham, appointed
Dean of Durham on his return, and Bishop Coverdale.
For some time these ardent reformers hoped that England might be brought into line with the Reformed

Churches on the Continent, but they were to be disappointed with the finality of the Elizabethan *via media*. As a result the Puritans came to be divided into two groups: the conforming Puritans who hoped, under auspicious circumstances, to reform the Church of England from within its ranks, and the non-conforming Puritans who demanded a 'reformation without tarrying for any'. The former were numerically powerful, as their Millenary Petition to the new monarch James I indicated, but in the course of time they either conformed completely, or threw in their lot with the non-conforming Puritans, Presbyterian or Independent, and with them set up clandestine churches, or sought asylum in the Low Countries or in the New England colonies.

The divergence between the Puritans and the clergy of the Establishment rested on a differing conception of the authority of the Word of God. The latter regarded the Bible as authoritative in matters of doctrine and conduct; whilst the former maintained that it contained the divine pattern for ecclesiastical government, worship, and discipline, as well as for belief. Hooker, for example, maintains that the outstanding ordinances of Christian worship are prescribed by the Bible, but that times, ceremonies, and circumstances are rightly to be decided by the rulers of the Church with due deference to the traditions of antiquity and the use of right reason. By contrast, the Puritan firmly held that the Word of God was authoritative for every aspect of ecclesiastical and common life. William Ames, distinguished theologian of the Puritans, writes of the Scriptures that 'they doe as well pertaine to the instructing of all the faithful through all ages, as if they had been specially directed to them'. He further adds that the Biblical revelation is binding in ecclesiastical government as it is in the regulation of behaviour: 'The Scripture is not partiall, but a perfect rule of faith and manners: neither is there here anything that is constantly and everywhere to be observed in the Church of God, which depends either upon tradition, or upon any authority whatsoever, and is not contained in the Scriptures.'[1]

The Puritan also differed from the clergy of the Establishment in his anthropology. The Anglican apologists were the upholders of the rights of human reason, believing that because revelation and reason are the gifts of the same Divine Author, everything revealed by God must be conformable to human reason. 'When both sides agree that these are the words of God', contends Jeremy Taylor, 'and the question of faith is concerning the meaning of the words, nothing is an article of faith, or a part of religion, but what can be proved by reason to be the sense and intentions of God.'[2] The Puritans objected that this was to make a faulty human instrument a judge over revelation. The human reason, as a consequence of the Fall, was distorted by original sin. Taylor appealed in vain to the treasured experience of antiquity, and the nobility of the human reason, for the Puritan knew the perversity of the human mind. He took his restatements of the doctrine of the authority of the Biblical revelation and of original sin from Calvin's Geneva. His mental journey, as a product of the Renaissance, might take him to Athens, but Geneva was his destination.

It was as a consequence of these beliefs that the Puritan stressed obedience to the divine revelation as the essential and primary virtue, that he regarded all

---

[1] *The Marrow of Sacred Divinity*, pp. 169–70.
[2] *Doctor Dubitantium* (ed. 1851), IX, 74.

man-made ceremonies and ritual in worship as sheer human impudence in the sight of God, that he worshipped not the impersonation of Truth, Beauty, and Goodness, but the omnipotent and holy God. 'The Lord reigneth, let the people tremble' was his motto. His God demanded unquestioning obedience in the way that He had declared His will in the Scriptures. Thus the Anglican's claim that the Church may institute ceremonies and customs, hallowed by antiquity and not prohibited by the Scriptures, seemed an affront to the divine majesty in the Puritan's eyes, apart from being a denial of the doctrine of original sin. Thus the Puritan liturgical reforms and the immense seriousness with which he accepted God's claim on his life, were not the idiosyncrasies of the heretic or proud schismatic, they were the proofs of his intense personal loyalty to God. He was no Pharisee who thanked God that he was not as other men are; rather he wished that all men might, like him, admit the sovereignty of God's sway in all departments of their life. He was no innovator; his complaint was that the Church from which he dissented had made unscriptural and therefore unauthorized innovations in her worship and government.

The Puritan insisted that the formal principle of the Reformation was adherence to the Word of God. The Fathers of the Church of England had applied the principle in doctrinal matters. Naturally and inevitably, he claimed, the second stage of Reformation in England was the application of the same criterion to the unreformed worship and government of the Church. Puritanism was therefore necessarily a liturgical movement. Positively, it wished to restore English worship to the simplicity, purity, and spirituality of the primitive Church, in which the chief liturgical notes were obedience and edification. Negatively, it wished to suppress those symbols in which a corrupt Romanism expressed its character. The latter accounts for the iconoclasm of Puritan worship.

The fear of Rome is comprehensible even at this distance of time; for the fires of Smithfield during Mary's persecution had not burnt out in the Puritan's memory. The drama of the Counter-Reformation was being played on the stage of his time. He feared that the adoption of the Roman symbols might make way for the adoption of the Roman substance. Hence he violently stigmatized the Roman ceremonies retained in the Book of Common Prayer as the 'badges of anti-Christ'. The use of the ring in marriage, 'crossing' in Baptism, kneeling at the reception of Holy Communion, the use of the surplice, were of their nature indifferent, neither commanded nor forbidden by the Word of God; but because of their associations with a powerful Church which would not be judged and reformed by the Word of God, they could not remain merely indifferent matters to him.

While Puritanism is, in the main, a liturgical movement, a further erosion of the medieval cliffs by the Reformation tides, it is more than that. It is a new religious attitude. Its ethos, integrating a profound loyalty to God with all the spheres of human existence, so that life itself is a prolonged act of adoration, is finely expressed by Lucy, the wife of Colonel Hutchinson: 'By Christianity I intend that universal habit of grace which is wrought in a soul by the regenerating Spirit of God, whereby the whole creature is resigned up into the Divine will and love, and all its actions designed to the obedience and glory of its Maker.'[1]

[1] *Memoirs of Colonel Hutchinson* (Everyman edition), p. 21.

This is what B. L. Manning called a heritage of 'intensity' in religion. Small wonder that the moderate, who mixed a small dose of Sunday religion with a great deal of weekday water, regarded the Puritans as fanatics, or religious maniacs. Yet the same heritage of intensity characterizes the chapel life of the twentieth century. Thomas Hardy may be taken as an unprejudiced witness of the grudging esteem in which the Puritan seriousness and sincerity were still held, almost two hundred years after the time of Lucy Hutchinson, in *Far from the Madding Crowd*.

'I believe ye be a chapel-member, Joseph,' says the innkeeper. ''That I do.'

'O, no, no. I don't go as far as that.'

'For my part, I'm staunch Church of England. . . .'

'Chapel-folk be more hand-in-glove with them above than we,' said Joseph thoughtfully.

'Yes,' said Coggan. 'We know very well that if anybody do go to heaven, they will. They've worked hard for it, and they deserve to have it, such as 'tis. I bain't such a fool as to pretend that we who stick to the Church have the same chance as they, because we know we have not.'

Along with the heritage of intensity in Dissent, there comes a heritage of simplicity, a pruning of the tree of faith to remove from it the fungus of the centuries. The weapon which made the necessary excisions was the Word of God 'sharper than any two-edged sword'. This lopping-off took many forms. The multitudinous holy-days of the medieval calendar were sacrificed so that the Sunday, the anniversary of our Lord's Resurrection, stood out in unrivalled glory. Hitherto, the medieval peak-days had been obscured by many low foot-hills of festivals; now the summit of the Lord's

Day stood majestically alone, dominating the religious landscape. In place of the seven medieval sacraments and superadded *sacramentalia*, the two dominical sacraments of the Word, Baptism and the Lord's Supper, reigned supreme and unchallenged. In place of the many mediators of the medieval church, the Blessed Virgin, the saints, the angels, and the priests, they claimed supremacy for our Lord, the sole Mediator between God and man. Worship and churchmanship were rescued from the complexities and corruptions that overlaid the Gospel.

In the third place, Puritanism widened the conception of 'sainthood' to its original New Testament sense, to include every servant of Christ. No longer was 'sainthood' the prerogative of celibates; it was the indisputable right of every Christian man, married or single, learned or simple, in Orders or out of Orders. Puritanism applied the Reformation and scriptural doctrine of 'the priesthood of all believers' to family-life and to ecclesiastical government. The father and head of every household was its priest, commissioned to lead family worship each morning and evening. The foundations of modern democracy are to be found in the Church Meetings of the Independents and Baptists, and the Class Meetings of the Methodists. For there simple men learned the art of Christian government. The form of ecclesiastical government was a Christocracy run by democrats, equal in the sight of God. Even in the more oligarchical type of government of the Presbyterians, the layman had a responsibility equal to that of the ministry. Lord Lindsay rightly claims this tradition of churchmanship as the progenitor of democratic government: 'Democracy is the application to social life of the principle of the spiritual priesthood of all believers. . . . If there cannot be free Churches except in a free State, there cannot be a free State unless there is in it a free Church.'[1]

Amongst the Puritans, the Independents and Baptists, rather than the Presbyterians, stood for a free and disestablished Church, though the Great Ejection of 1662 under the Clarendon Code forced the three denominations to take a common platform. This was due to their recognition that religion is, though communally transmitted, a personal and individual transaction between man and his Maker. Hence, the Puritans preferred to express their faith in terms of Covenants rather than of Creeds, in terms of declarations of loyalty to Christ and His Church, rather than of intellectual affirmations. Hence, too, the recognition in Puritanism (in words of a Victorian poet) that

> There is no expeditious road
> To pack and label men for God,
> And save them by the barrel-load.

It is no accident that caused the Puritans to describe their religious communities as 'gathered Churches'; the very term indicated that the members had been chosen by God out of the world to fulfil His purpose. A State Church meant a nominal Christianity and a coercive religion. Thus, a by-product of Puritanism was a concern for toleration. Roger Williams finds it in his heart to plead for the Roman Catholics suffering under disabilities, in the words: 'An arm of flesh and sword of steel cannot reach to cut the darkness of the mind, the hardness and unbelief of the heart, and kindly operate on the soul's affections to forsake a long-continued father's worship, and to embrace a new,

[1] *The Churches and Democracy*, pp. 31 and 74.

B

though the truest and the best.' [1] It was the recognition of the worth of the individual as a person for whom Christ had died that produced freedom of conscience. This Puritan flower is found growing on the soil of Independency as early as 1645 in a tract entitled *The Ancient Bounds*. Christ's words are represented thus: ' "Return into the scabbard," says He to the magistrate's sword, "I will have none of thee to cut the way for my truth, through woods and rocks and mountains, through stony hearts and implicated reasonings. Not by might, not by power, but by my Spirit, saith the Lord." ' [2]

One further consequence of Puritanism, indeed an unexpected one, must not be omitted. This is the Puritan's love for education. The criticism of the pretensions of human reason inherent in the doctrine of original sin, might have led to philistinism in the arts and sciences. On the other hand, Reformed theologians were the products of the universities, and the arch-theologian of Puritanism, John Calvin, was careful to insist that human reason, though an imperfect instrument for the apprehension of divine revelation until regenerate, was entirely adequate for other human necessities. [3] The leaders of Puritanism were men of high academic distinction: Cartwright, the father of English Presbyterianism, was Lady Margaret Professor of Divinity at Cambridge during Elizabeth's reign, and in Commonwealth days, when the Puritan centre had been transferred to the sister university, the Independent John Owen was Vice-Chancellor and Dean of Christ Church, whilst another Independent, Thomas Goodwin, was President of Magdalen. Indeed, if the

[1] A. S. P. Woodhouse, *Puritanism and Liberty*, p. 288.
[2] *op. cit.*, p. 263.   [3] *Institutes*, Bk. I.

incarnation of culture and religion in one man is sought, the palm goes to John Milton, poet, Foreign Secretary, and Puritan. A recent tribute to the educational enthusiasm of the Puritans asserts:

> The greatness of the Puritans is not so much that they conquered a wilderness, or that they carried a religion into it, but that they carried a religion which . . . was nevertheless indissolubly bound up with an ideal of culture and learning. In contrast to all other pioneers, they made no concession to the forest, but in the midst of frontier conditions, in the very throes of clearing the land and erecting shelters, they maintained schools and a college, a standard of scholarship and competent writing, a class of men devoted entirely to the life of the mind and the soul.[1]

Whilst these words refer to the Puritan emigrants to New England, where they established the universities of Yale and Harvard, they apply equally to the English Puritans. It is, for instance, doubtful if a more distinguished gathering of educated ecclesiastics than the Westminster Assembly of Divines has ever been held in England. The same zeal for education was maintained under the almost insuperable difficulties caused by the Clarendon Code in the Nonconformist Dissenting Academies. These were manned by the Fellows and Tutors of Oxford and Cambridge who were ejected for their Puritan convictions at the Restoration, and they outstripped the ancient universities in the teaching of science and modern languages. True to the same tradition was George Whitefield, who, a century later, was either to found or to further the progress of Kingswood School, Bath, Doddridge's Academy, Northampton, and Harvard and Dartmouth Colleges in New

[1] Miller and Johnson, *The Puritans* (New York, 1938), p. 11.

England. In addition, he encouraged the growth of Log College which, when transplanted to Princeton, became the mother of the modern Princeton University; whilst his charity school at Philadelphia developed into the University of Pennsylvania. The same concern for higher education was to be developed in the foundation of Sunday and day schools in late eighteenth-century England. Here, again, the Church—and particularly the Free Churches—had anticipated the State, as also in the case of philanthropic and social enterprises. It may be safely conjectured that the Puritan's zeal for educational advance was a correlate of his belief in the significance of the individual for whom Christ died. Education was not for the privileged few, but for all who could benefit by it.

The foregoing, it may be said, is a rose-coloured picture of the Puritan. What of the more sombre tints in the portraiture? The Puritan must be drawn, as the Protector requested for himself, 'warts and all'. It must be admitted that his love of the Bible became bibliolatry, when he sought within its covers for sartorial guidance, or for political direction. It must be recognized that his zeal outran his discretion, that his righteousness often degenerated into self-righteousness, and that his ecclesiastical discipline purified the Church sometimes at the cost of making it priggish. It must be recorded that individual Puritans were philistines in art and music, iconoclastic in liturgy, and hard taskmasters in business. Its successes were the sense of the individual's responsibility to God, and the recognition of divine standards for conduct, and of the need for the redemption of man and society, with the by-products enumerated above. Puritanism failed because it hid the fact that the physical pleasures are,

within limits, good, and because its exaltation of the
economic virtues produced a neglect of contemplation
and conversation, thus creating a profound dissatisfaction with life. The Puritan theocracy could only
succeed where all men were regenerate; where they
were not, 'the reign of the saints' was loathed with
unimaginable vehemence. The successes of Puritanism
have passed into the life-stream of the English Free
Churches; its failures have been discarded, except by
the controversialist. Behind the failure of Puritanism
as a way of life, there was a theological mistake: the
sons of Calvin had overemphasized the retributive
justice of God to the overshadowing of the divine love,
with the consequence of sanctioning vengefulness in
human affairs.

Such was the tradition that moulded the religious and
political life of the seventeenth and subsequent centuries of English history. But whence came Puritanism
to England? A clue is provided in the scurrilous creed
attributed to the Puritans by their opponents of the
Establishment, which reads:

I believe in *John Calvin*, the Father of our Religion,
Disposer of Heaven and Earth, and in *Owen, Baxter*, and
Jenkins his deare Sons our Lords, who were conceived
by the Spirit of Fanaticism, born of Schism and Faction,
suffered under the *Act of Uniformity*.[1]

The spiritual father of the Puritans was indeed John
Calvin, and their spiritual home was Geneva, the city
which John Knox had glowingly apostrophized as 'the
most perfect school of the Apostles since the time of
Christ'. If the first stage of the Reformation was the
Lutheran rediscovery of the Gospel, the second stage

[1] *The Presbyterian Pater-Noster*, a broadsheet of 1681, now
in the Bodleian Library.

was the rediscovery of churchmanship which was accomplished in the Genevan theocracy. In this *cité des étrangers*, with 6,000 exiles swelling the normal population of 13,000, Calvin directed the theology and the strategy of the Protestant resistance movements in the Catholic countries of Europe. The ministry of the Reformed Churches was trained at the newly established University of Geneva in his *Institutio Christianae Religionis*, whilst the ordinary church member was taught in the Catechism of Calvin's composing to give a reason for his faith. Here, too, was perfected the well-balanced and finely disciplined system of church government, subsequently known as Presbyterianism. Perhaps the greatest achievement of all was to turn this dissolute city into the admiration of the Christian world. These bare facts alone help to explain the nostalgia of the Puritan for Geneva. It was his *Civitas Dei*. Calvin's Geneva was the *fons et origo* of Puritanism, and of its impetus for further 'Reformation according to the Word of God'.

How, then, was Calvinistic Puritanism transmitted to England? It was mediated by persons and writings. In the main the persons who were the apostles of Calvinism were exiles, either Continental exiles who found an asylum from persecution in the days of Edward VI, or returning English exiles who had left England during the time of Henry VIII or Queen Mary and returned in more auspicious days. The writings which acted as the *media* of Calvinism were both the Genevan liturgical compilations and the important Genevan Bible, with its theological marginal comments.

In the reign of Edward VI the ancient universities, by the wish of Cranmer, invited two distinguished Reformers to occupy the Regius chairs of Divinity;

Martin Bucer went to Cambridge and Peter Martyr to
Oxford. Bucer was Calvin's predecessor at Strasbourg,
and his order of worship for the church was the foundation of Calvin's Strasbourg Liturgy. Whilst Bucer was
a mediator between Luther and Calvin, he may in this
connexion be regarded as Calvin's forerunner in England. His influence preceded his arrival, for in 1547
there appeared in an English translation the liturgical
and doctrinal instrument of Reformation prepared by
him and Melancthon for Hermann, Archbishop of
Cologne, which was to have a profound influence on
the Book of Common Prayer as revised in 1552. When
in England, moreover, he prepared a series of careful
animadversions or 'Certayn Notes' on the Communion
Order of that Liturgy. Furthermore, it was a loyal
disciple of Calvin, John Knox, who was responsible for
the introduction of the 'Black Rubric' into that prayer
book, which excluded the notion of 'anye reall and
essencial presence there beeynge of Christ's naturall
fleshe and bloude' in the Sacrament. Calvin's influence
on the most Puritan of the English Church formularies
may be summed up as follows: the Sentences, the
Exhortation, the Confession and Absolution, in the
Daily Service of the 1552 book were borrowed from
Calvin's Strasbourg Liturgy; he may also be responsible indirectly for the introduction of the Decalogue
into the Order for Communion, as his disciple Pullain
was for the responses to the Decalogue; the words of
administration are taken from the Calvinist Liturgy of
John a Lasco, who in turn borrowed them from the
Strasbourg Liturgy. In addition, Calvin's influence
was mediated by Bishop John Hooper of Gloucester,
who had been an exile in the Reformed Churches of
the Continent during Henry VIII's reign, and who

inaugurated the Vestiarian Controversy, basing his objection to the use of vestments on the sufficiency of the Word of God as the directory for ceremonial.

Of even greater importance are the second group of exiles, who took refuge in the Low Countries or in Switzerland during the Marian persecution, for amongst them we find the two groups of Puritans: the right-wing and the left-wing Puritans. The account of their disagreement in liturgical matters at Frankfort anticipates the inevitable struggle between conforming and non-conforming Puritans in Elizabethan England, in addition to providing evidence of the *media* of the transmission of Calvinism to England. The document which provided this interesting prophecy of the shape of things to come is entitled *A Brief Discourse of the Troubles begun at Frankfort in the year 1554 about the Book of Common Prayer and Ceremonies*.[1] The dispute, to state it briefly, concerned the provision of an adequate formulary for the exiles of Frankfort. One party, the Knoxians, were eager to use a revised translation of Calvin's Genevan Order, which afterwards became known as *John Knox's Genevan Service Book*. The other party, the Coxians, were adamant in their desire to retain the 1552 Prayer Book,

least by much altering of the same we should seem to condemn the chief authors thereof, who, as they now suffer, so are they ready to confirm that fact with the price of their bloods and should also both give occasion to our adversaries to accuse our doctrine of imperfection and us of mutability and the godly to doubt in that truth wherein before they were persuaded and to hinder their coming hither which before they had purposed.[2]

[1] Reprinted (ed. Arber), 1909.
[2] *op. cit.*, p. xxiii.

The Knoxians, for their part, could not feel that all the ceremonies in the 1552 book were warranted by the Word of God, and they were strengthened in their resolve not to use it by Calvin's opinion that the formulary contained 'many allowable but foolish things'. The importance of the divergence of opinion represented by the two parties is that, when they returned to England in the opening days of Elizabeth's reign, the one party fought for a reintroduction of the 1552 book and the other asserted the claims of the Genevan order. Thus the conflict within the Establishment was joined four years before Elizabeth succeeded to the throne. Moreover, Whittingham, one of the Knoxian party, appointed to the Deanery of Durham by Elizabeth, became one of the protagonists of the left-wing Puritans. A further consequence of the 'Frankfort Troubles' was that the radical Puritans, dissatisfied with the Book of Common Prayer, used the Genevan Service Book in their services, as Strype records.[1] Moreover, the Knoxian criticisms of the Anglican Prayer Book provided the left-wing Puritans with a strong armoury from which they drew weapons for attacking it as not being 'according to the Word of God'. Luther, it may be said, had held that what is not explicitly forbidden by the Word of God may be permitted in Christian worship, whereas Calvin insisted on a Scriptural warrant for ritual and ceremonial. It was because of this divergent view of the authority of the Word of God in liturgy that the Coxians and the Knoxians, the conforming and non-conforming Puritans, were separated.

The other notable medium of Calvinism in England

[1] Strype's *Grindal*, p. 168, p. 203; Strype's *Parker*, II, p. 265; Strype's *Whitgift*, I, p. 348.

was the Genevan Bible, in which William Whittingham appears to have played the part of chief translator. The New Testament was issued in 1557, the Psalms in 1559, and the Bible in 1560. This was the popular Bible of Elizabethan England, only to be supplanted by the Authorized Version of 1611. Its importance as a transmitter of Puritanism lies in its often tendentious glosses, and the prologue to the first edition prepared by Calvin himself. The following may be taken as typical examples of Puritan glosses in the Genevan Bible. The Establishment was attacked in the comment on Deuteronomy vii. 5: 'God would have His service pure without all idolatrous ceremonies and superstitutions.' The Puritan plea for extemporary prayer found expression in the annotation of Matthew vi. 9 (on the Lord's Prayer): 'Christ bindeth them not to the words, but to the sense and form of prayer.' Calvinist sacramental theology is taught in the marginal note on John xx. 17 (on Mary Magdalene at the open tomb): 'Because she was so much addicted to ye corporall presence, Christ teacheth her to lift up her mind by faith into heaven where we sit with him at the right hand of the Father.' In these words, it may be noted, there is exact verbal correspondence with the Exhortation in Calvin's Genevan Communion Order. The ecclesiastical hierarchy was attacked in the elucidation of the meaning of Revelation ix. 3 (describing the locusts emerging from the smoke) as 'Hereticks, false Teachers, worldly, subtle, prelates, with Monks, Fryars, Cardinals, Patriarchs, Archbishops, Bishops, Doctors, Batchelors and Masters.' The Genevan Bible was, it will be seen, a polemical handbook for the Puritan attack on the Establishment, literally with chapter and verse for every contention based upon the ground of the

Word of God. Its theology and its popularity were the twin dangers of the Establishment from the Puritan quarter. Another important source of Protestant and even of Puritan propaganda was John Foxe's *Actes and Monuments* (commonly known as 'The Book of Martyrs'). This member of the Genevan party in Frankfort reminded complacent Protestants that theirs was a blood-bought faith.

By these media the Puritans in England were fortified to prepare for the battle for further Reformation 'according to the Word of God'. For them the Bible superseded any claim of the Church as interpreter, or as the custodian of authoritative tradition. This was the forefront of the Puritan attack on the Establishment in Cartwright's days; the strategy had not changed when Milton, sixty years later, supporting the Presbyterian attack on the Prelacy, challenged his opponents in the words:

Let them chant while they will of prerogatives, we shall tell them of Scripture; of custom, we of Scripture; of Acts and Statutes, still of Scripture, till the quick and piercing word enter to the dividing of their souls, and the mighty weakness of the Gospel throw down the weak mightiness of man's reasoning. Wherefore should we not urge only the Gospel, and hold it ever in their faces like a mirror of diamond till it dazzle and pierce their misty eyeballs? Maintaining it the honour of its absolute sufficiency and supremacy inviolable.

If *sola fide* was the watchword of the Lutheran Reformation, *sola Scriptura* was the password of the Puritan revolutionaries.

CHAPTER II

CONFORMING AND
NON-CONFORMING PURITANS

THE accession of Elizabeth was hailed with joy both by
the Marian refugees who hastened back from the Continent and by the majority of Englishmen who feared
Mary's marital and political alliance with Spain. The
latter were to be satisfied, even enthusiastic; the former
were to be disappointed. The truth was that Elizabeth's
religious policy was subservient to her political aim of
national unity. She deliberately chose to make Canterbury independent of Rome and Geneva, with the result
that Jesuit priests and Puritan preachers alike were persecuted under the Elizabethan settlement, as potential
enemies of England's unity.

Just as in troubled Frankfort there was a party for
further Reformation which was loyal to the Edwardian
Establishment, and another group that pressed for
greater conformity with the Genevan settlement, so in
troubled Elizabethan England there were conforming
and non-conforming Puritans. Their aims were the
same, but their methods different. The conforming
Puritans hoped for a further Reformation according
to the Word of God, to be established by constitutional
means, by the machinery of Parliament. The non-conforming Puritans, more impatient, less sanguine of the
prospects of constitutional reform, determined to have
'a Reformation without tarrying for any'.[1] At the first
there was little to distinguish the two parties, since it

[1] This phrase is the title of a book by Robert Browne.

appeared that the second stage of Reformation might be accomplished, as the conforming Puritans desired, in the first zeal of the anti-Marian reaction. It was only as the Elizabethan enactments of uniformity multiplied and were more stringently applied that the non-conforming Puritans emerged as the separate and impatient party. The controversy of the Puritans with the Establishment appears to have developed in two stages.

The first phase of the struggle is known as the 'Vestiarian Controversy'. All Puritans, remembering the stand of Bishop Hooper in the days of 'that blessed ympe', Edward VI, were united in condemning the 'idolatrous gear' that was imposed on all the clergy by the royal command. The first of the Acts of Uniformity was promulgated in 1559, by which the Edwardian Prayer Book of 1552, with its rubrics, was re-established as the liturgical standard of the realm. In the same year Parliament was persuaded to pass the Act of Supremacy, and each of the clergy was required to make the following avowal of allegiance:

I, A. B., do utterly testify and declare in my conscience, that the queen's highness is the only supreme governor of this realm, and of all other her highness's dominions and countries, as well in all spiritual or ecclesiastical things or causes, as temporal, . . .[1]

The oath was to be sworn 'upon the evangelist', without consideration that its claim that the Queen was spiritually 'supreme governor' might be itself a contradiction of the Gospel, or an infringement of the rights of Christ as the true Head of the Church or of the liberty of the Christian believer. Over two hundred clergy, and a few bishops, refused the oath and were deprived of their offices. If the voice of the Puritans is not yet heard

[1] Bettenson, *Documents of the Christian Church*, p. 330.

in articulate protest, it is probably because they interpreted the new enactments less as an infringement of the Christian subject's liberties than as a denial of Papal interference.

It appears that the Act of Uniformity was not strenuously applied at first. For some years a number of irregularities were noticed in the conduct of public worship. Whilst some desired and were prepared to wait for a purer worship and more stringent ecclesiastical discipline, others within the national Church took the law into their own hands. Variations from the liturgical norm observed at the time included: the disuse of the surplice in leading worship; the removal of the communion-table from the chancel to the body of the church, and the reception of the elements sitting, instead of kneeling; and the refusal to make the sign of the cross over infants during baptism. Opposition and irregularities continued for several years, growing in volume and defiance. The Puritans, led by a number of distinguished clergy, presented a petition to Convocation in 1563, demanding the abolition of the offending vestments and the 'noxious' ceremonies. The strength of the representation and its influence may be gathered from the result: the Puritans were defeated by one vote. Now that constitutional means of remedy had been overthrown, some Puritans had a clear conscience in establishing their own purer worship. The general chaos demanded disciplinary action and this Archbishop Parker, apparently on his own authority, attempted to apply in the Advertisements of 1566. This was an endeavour to enforce the minimum of uniformity in liturgical practice: the official Homilies were prescribed in lieu of sermons of the incumbent's own composition; surplices were insisted upon, whilst in collegiate and cathedral churches copes were to be worn for the celebration of the Holy Communion, and hoods on all other occasions; and the invariable posture for communicants was to be kneeling. Instantly objections were raised by the Puritans, under the guidance of the President of Magdalen and the Dean of Christ Church, Oxford. They condemned the vestments and ceremonies as 'the badges of Anti-Christ', the superstitious relics of a superseded faith. Parker, with the Bishop of London, cited the clergy of that city to appear before him at Lambeth, and to subscribe. Thirty-seven of the hundred-and-ten who appeared refused to conform. Their action marks the beginning of organized Puritanism in England.

The second stage of Puritan controversy is characterized by a more comprehensive and detailed attack upon the Book of Common Prayer. The ground moved from controversies over ceremonial and vestments to disputes over order and discipline. The very rigour of the enforcement of the Elizabethan settlement led to a more thorough-going challenge of the Erastianism of the State-Church. This, in turn, led to Separatism and its conception of 'the gathered Church' and the demand for religious toleration.

The Puritans, driven from their pulpits, preached against the Establishment in pamphlets of unrestrained vigour. A flood of criticism of the Prayer Book was in full spate. It was meticulously subjected to examination according to the Puritan's supreme liturgical criterion, the Word of God. What began as an objection to vestments and ceremonies was now magnified into a criticism of a formulary of prayer as such, and of the disastrous spiritual effects of enforcing homilies and forms of prayer on the ministry of the Church. It was, moreover, in the formulation of detailed criticisms on the existing form of worship that the Puritans were led to seek for more satisfactory alternatives. The suppression of Puritanism within the Establishment led to the increase of Separatism. But a large party remained within the national Church, refusing to contemplate schism, and hoping for a change of heart in the sovereign or, if that seemed unlikely, a change of sovereign. The strength of the conforming Puritans is evident in the Millenary petition they presented to James I soon after his accession. Indeed, the conforming party did not lose heart from the equivocal replies of 'the wisest fool in Christendom' but maintained their Puritan convictions in silence, or left with the Pilgrim Fathers in 1620 for New England, as a better alternative to schism. These, the gentler spirits, were only bludgeoned into revolution, by the intransigeance of Laud and the absolutism of Charles.

During all these years they engaged only in literary warfare, but all the time they were erecting a mental alternative system of church government and worship, whilst the Separatists built their concrete substitutes for the Establishment. During this second phase of the Puritan controversy, the conforming Puritans did not abate their criticism of the Book of Common Prayer, nor cease to plead for a purer worship and government based on the Word of God, and the practice of the apostolic Church. Unwearyingly they urged that 2 Pet. i. 19–21 and 2 Tim. iii. 15–17 assert the perfection of the Scriptures; that Matt. xv. 9, 13, Rev. xxii. 18–19, and Exod. xx. 4–6 (the Second Commandment) prohibited man-made additions to the Word of God. Having maintained their thesis, they then proceeded to examine the Scriptures for evidences of the worship which God demands from His people. They believed that true worship according to the will of God is found in six ordinances: (i) Prayer, (ii) Praise, (iii) Preaching, (iv) the administration of the Sacraments of Baptism and the Lord's Supper, (v) catechizing, and (vi) the exercise of ecclesiastical discipline.

Their authority for types of prayer was the apostolic injunction in 1 Tim. ii. 1 ff. which authorized petition, thanksgiving, and intercession, whilst the Lord's Prayer sanctioned adoration and confession. The Biblical warrant for the preference of standing to kneeling in prayer was the example of Abraham (Gen. xviii. 22) and the words of our Lord (Mark xi. 25). Responsive prayers were vetoed by the Word of God, they claimed, in Neh. viii. 6 and 1 Cor. xiv. 14–16.

As for Praise, the Puritans re-established the importance of praises as the liturgical offering of the whole congregation, not merely of the choir. Their warrants were the Psalms and the New Testament injunctions to praise God 'with psalms and hymns and spiritual songs, singing and making melody in your heart to the Lord' (Eph. v. 19). It was also their custom, on the authority of Matt. xxvi. 30, to conclude the celebration of the Lord's Supper with a psalm.

The central feature of Puritan worship was the sermon. It was the declaration of God's saving truth to His people. No homily, in their judgement, could fulfil the task of expounding the Word and applying it to the hearts of the congregation. To insist on homilies instead of sermons, was to make the ministers into 'dumb dogges'. The importance of preaching was stressed by the whole corpus of the Scriptures, prophetic and apostolic, but particularly by 2 Cor. i. 12, and Rom. x. 14–15.

C

The Puritans accepted only two sacraments as of dominical institution: Baptism and the Lord's Supper. Their sacramental theology, as their administration of the sacraments, rested upon the apostolic practice. They always recited the institution narrative in the Lord's Supper as their warrant for the ordinance (1 Cor. xi. 23 ff.), and they invariably prefaced the rite of Baptism with the recitation of Matt. xxviii. 19 f. They interpreted 'Do this in remembrance of me' as a command to repeat the original order of the manual and spiritual actions of Christ. Similarly, as Jesus had received little children, so they also took them into their arms to baptize them. They believed that they were adhering faithfully to the dominical institution in the administration of both the 'gospel sacraments'.

As will become apparent later, the Puritans objected to set forms of prayer (liturgies) and preaching (homilies), so that they had to justify the use of a set catechism. They found the necessary proof-text in 2 Tim. i. 13: 'Hold fast the *form of sound words* which thou hast heard of me, in faith and love which is in Christ Jesus.' Another Puritan ordinance, which has affinity with catechizing, was 'prophesying'. This means of expounding the Scriptures and clearing up obscurities and objections was a favourite holy exercise among them. Their warrant for this was found in verses 31 and 1 of 1 Cor. xiv., which justified even the plurality of prophets.

The sixth ordinance was known as 'Ecclesiastical Discipline' or 'Ecclesiastical Censures'. Its purpose was to cut off the decaying or dead branches from the trunk of the Church, and thus maintain its purity. Apostolic authority for this practice was discovered in the example of the excommunication of Simon Magus by St. Peter (Acts viii. 13) and of the incestuous person by St. Paul (1 Cor. v. 1–7). The complete procedure for admonition, excommunication, and restoration, when penitent, was founded on Matt. xviii. 15–18.

The Puritans found in the Word of God the proto-types of their occasional, as well as of their regular ordinances. For instance, if they held a day of humilia-tion for the repentance of the people (a fairly frequent event in Commonwealth times), the invariable order of procedure was fasting, prayer, and sermon (as in Acts xiii. 1–3, and xiv. 2).

This may, at first sight, be dismissed as unintelligent exegesis, perhaps even the search for biblical rationaliza-tions. Occasionally mere ingenuity, even perversity, overpowers spiritual insight, as when Thomas Cart-wright argues for the retention of the same locality and posture in divine worship (as over against Anglican movements and processions) from the words: 'Peter stood up in the midst of the disciples'.[1] On the other hand, their opponents could cite Scripture for their own purposes. The latter were not above defending prostra-tion at the name of Jesus on the warrant of Phil. ii. 10, on which Calderwood pithily observes: 'Cur magis ad titulos Filii quam Patris aut Spiritus Sancti?'[2] On the whole, it was the spirit rather than the letter of the Scripture that the Puritans observed. If the clergy of the Establishment defend the use of the surplice with Rev. xv. 6 as their proof-text, the Puritans argue for the abolition of vestments associated with the Roman Church on the grounds that they are Aaronical and unsuited therefore to the New Dispensation, that they are badges of idolatry, that they do not edify, and that they are a stumbling-block to the weaker brethren. In

[1] Acts i. 15.   [2] *Altare Damascenum* (1623), p. 623.

this they follow the purport of the Epistle to the Hebrews and Rom. xiv. 15, and not least, our Lord's *caveat* against the Pharisees who wished to be esteemed for their long garments (Matt. xxiii. 5-7).

On the question of ceremonies, the Anglicans urged tradition, but the Puritans contended that the essence of Christian freedom from the Law is that Christians should not be burdened by unnecessary traditions, claiming that the Epistle to the Galatians and Acts xv. 28 were on their side. In the matter of kneeling for the reception of Communion, the Puritans desired to 'avoid the appearance of evil' (1 Thess. v. 22), i.e. the suggestion of transubstantiation and the adoration of the elements. Foremost in the liturgical controversy was the question whether set forms or free prayers were acceptable to God. The Anglicans found numerous warrants for set forms of prayer in the Scriptures,[1] but the Puritans preferred to rely on the consensus of New Testament teaching which insisted that 'the Spirit helpeth our infirmities' (Rom. viii. 26-7). A pneumatic and a legal worship were incompatible, they held. They equated set forms of worship with tutelage under the Law, and a pneumatic worship, utilizing free prayers inspired by the Spirit, with the liberty of the New Dispensation under Christ.

The contest was of more than local or ephemeral interest; the Puritans could have retorted that their opponents of the Establishment, not they, were insular. It was the constant plea of the Puritans that Anglican worship should be brought into conformity with that of the other Reformed Churches. The perennial interest of the controversy lies in the Puritan's loyalty to the Biblical revelation, and in the by-products of his

[1] e.g. Exod. xv. 1; Num. vi. 23-6; Hos. xiv. 1-3.

passion for liberty to obey the dictates of his God. It
is this combination of personal integrity in religion and
life, with the demand for liberty, at the personal cost
of imprisonment, exile, or emigration, that constitutes
the Puritan's claim on the gratitude and pious remembrance of succeeding generations.

In the years immediately succeeding the promulga-
tion of the Advertisements, there is evidence for the
existence of two distinct groups within the Puritans,
the one within the Establishment, the other outside it.
In 1567 the non-conforming Puritans formed a
'gathered church' which met at Plumbers Hall. When
its members were cited to appear before the new Archbishop, Edmund Grindal, they made the following
apologia:

> So long as we might have the Word freely preached
> and the Sacraments administered without the preferring
> of idolatrous gear about it, we never assembled together
> in houses. But when it came to this, that all our preachers
> were displaced by your law, so that we could hear none
> of them in any Church by the space of seven or eight
> weeks, and were troubled and commanded by your
> courts from day to day for not coming to our parish
> churches, then we bethought us what were best to do.
> And now if from the Word of God, you can prove we
> are wrong, we will yield to you and do open penance at
> St. Paul's Cross; if not, we will stand to it by the grace
> of God.[1]

This group did not desire to remain permanently
separated from the Establishment; they were forced
into temporary non-conformity, until the offensive
enactments of the Queen should be repealed. The

[1] Burrage, *Early English Dissenters* (1912), Chap. II.

views of Puritans of this group were greatly strengthened by the formidable attack on the Established
Church contained in the Puritan manifesto entitled the
First Admonition. This lengthy pamphlet presented
the findings of a group of Puritan ministers who had
met in conference in London, and who now desired to
make recommendations for the consideration of Parliament. They take exception not only to the worship of
the Establishment, but to its ecclesiastical government.
They plead for the removal of a ministry of bishops,
priests, and deacons, and the substitution of a ministry
of pastors, elders, and deacons, in conformity with
apostolic precedent. Furthermore, they maintain that
the minister should be invited to, not forced upon, the
Church in which he is to exercise his ministry. This
provoked a reply from Whitgift, in which he defended
the Establishment on the ground of the ancient traditions of the undivided Church. There followed a
Second Admonition, more trenchant than the first,
penned by Thomas Cartwright, with the delineation of
a truly Reformed Church in liturgy and government.
The latter he envisaged on the Genevan model, with
a party of elected ministers, governing through conferences, synods, and consistories. The consistories were
to have powers of excommunication and moral supervision, and their representatives were to attend the
synods and conferences. This was, in effect, a plea for
a Presbyterian system. It received short shrift from
the authorities, but there is evidence that a number of
local churches made voluntary associations of the kind
envisaged by Cartwright, whilst 'prophesyings' for the
better instruction of the clergy were instituted in many
parts of the country. Indeed, these were only forbidden when Archbishop Grindal had been virtually

deprived of his authority and confined to his palace by
the Queen for his defence of these proceedings. It was
the logical outcome of the *Admonitions* that resulted in
the establishment of the first Presbyterian Church at
Wandsworth in 1572.

Meanwhile, the second group of Puritans, the nonconformists, had been setting up their Separatist 'conventicles' in England, born of the impatience of 'reformation without tarrying for any'. Their importance
is twofold: firstly, they provided the concrete alternatives to the established ways of worship and government, whilst the conforming Puritans had only paper
alternatives to offer; secondly, their freedom from
ecclesiastical traditions enabled them to make liturgical
experiments, from which the conforming Puritans were
to benefit in Commonwealth days. It is important to
notice that, apart from their radical divergence in their
attitude towards the State Church, Puritans and
Separatists were largely in agreement. The term
'Separatists' is not applied to the Independents, because
they stoutly denied its validity in their *Apologeticall
Narration* presented to the Westminster Assembly of
Divines, but it is a convenient description of the
Barrowists, the Brownists, and the Anabaptists of
Elizabethan times.

The Barrowists flourished from 1587 to 1593, and
their leaders, Barrowe himself, Greenwood, and Penry,
all died for their faith. Their liturgical importance is
that they denied the validity of all set forms of prayer,
in contradistinction to the Puritans who employed
liturgies and whose objection to the Book of Common
Prayer was based, in the first instance, on such contents
as were without Biblical warrant, rather than on the
fact that it was a formulary of worship. They also

appear to have anticipated the Puritans in the holding of 'prophesyings' for it is recorded that they assembled in the fields bordering London at 5 a.m. and ' . . . they contynewe in there kinde of praier and exposicion of Scriptures all that daie'.[1] Their administration of the Sacraments was simplicity itself, for they did away with godparents or sponsors and merely pronounced the infants baptized in the triune name after sprinkling. The Barrowist Lord's Supper is characterized by the same simplicity and fidelity to the Scriptural account of institution. The pastor blessed five white loaves and, after reading the appropriate account of the inauguration of the Lord's Supper, broke the bread and delivered it to his neighbour, who, having broken off a piece of bread, passed it to his neighbour in turn. Similarly, the cup was blessed, and handed on from neighbour to neighbour, until all had communicated. In the matter of ecclesiastical discipline, in regarding marriage as a purely civil contract, and burials as civil and not ecclesiastical ceremonies, as well as in their use of covenants, there is little doubt that the Separatists provided the Puritans with the precedent for their characteristic usages.

The Brownists, under their leader Robert Browne, a former clergyman in the Establishment, achieved complete separation in Norwich in 1581. Browne's popularity, however, brought him to the notice of the authorities, and he and his company moved to Middelburg in the following year. Their worship seems to have been identical with that of the Barrowists, but Browne's significance lies in the sphere of church government rather than in liturgy. He maintained that the first principle of churchmanship is that the

[1] Burrage, *op. cit.*, I, p. 26.

Church shall consist only of Christians, in his famous definition:

The Church planted or gathered is a company or number of Christians or believers, which, by a willing convenant made with their God, are under the government of God and Christ, and keep his laws in one holy communion: because Christ hath redeemed them unto holiness and happiness for ever, from which they were fallen by the sin of Adam.[1]

Here we find the origin of the Puritan inheritance of intensity in religion, that scorns a merely nominal membership of a Church; here, too, is expressed the priesthood of all believers, since they, not the hierarchy, rule the Church under Christ; here, again, is the seed-plot of democratic government. While all Puritans were to be debtors to Robert Browne, the Independents and Baptists look to him as the pioneer of their system of church government.

The Anabaptists appear to have had no organized existence until 1612, though they are encountered sporadically as individuals. The home of English Anabaptism is Holland, where it appears to have emerged as an offshoot of the Barrowists or Brownists. The first known English Baptist congregation seems to be that over which Thomas Helwys presided in 1612, which withdrew from John Smyth's congregation in Amsterdam. The characteristic difference between the Anabaptists and the other Separatists concerned the mode of administering and the recipients of Baptism. Helwys insisted upon believer's baptism, either by immersion or sprinkling, as a necessity for salvation. He even declared that the practice of infant baptism was

[1] *A Booke which sheweth the Life and Manners of all true Christians, ad loc.*

sufficient to warrant eternal damnation, ' . . . if you had
no other sin amongst you al, but this, you perish everie
man off you from the highest to the lowest, iff you
repent not'.[1] How far the Anabaptists went in the
direction of free and pneumatic worship may be seen in
the following account given by Smyth in 1608:

> Wee hould that the worship of the new testament
> properly so called is spirituall proceeding originally from
> the hart: & that reading out of a booke (though lawfull
> eclesiastical action) is no part of spirituall worship, but
> rather the invention of the man of synne it beeing sub-
> stituted for a part of spirituall worship. Wee hould that
> seeing prophesiing is a parte of spirituall worship; there-
> fore in time of prophesjng it is vnlawfull to have the
> booke as a helpe before the eye. Wee hould that seeing
> singinging [sic] a psalme is a parte of spirituall worship
> therefore it is vnlawfull to have the booke before the eye
> in time of singinge a psalme.[2]

In this type of worship 'in the Spirit' the Anabaptists
appear to be the forerunners of the Quakers in the
rejection of forms and symbols. It also appears that
the Anabaptists despised singing in unison, as a denial
of spiritual spontaneity, allowing only soloists in their
services. This tradition lasted as late as 1690 amongst
the English Baptists, since Benjamin Keach, the
pioneer hymn-writer of the Free Churches, had great
difficulty in persuading his Baptist congregation in
Horsleydown to sing in unison. We have seen that
Helwys allowed immersion or sprinkling as modes of
administering believer's baptism; but immersion exclusively was insisted upon by the London Baptists in

[1] Burrage, op. cit., I, 253.
[2] The Differences of the Churches of the Separation (1605),
p. v.

1633, under the leadership of Jessey and Blunt, 'being convinced of Baptism, yt also ought to be by diping ye Body into ye Water, resembling Burial and rising again.' [1]

Marriage was sanctioned by the early Baptists only if the contracting parties belonged to their communion. There is evidence that they held love-feasts as a general feature of their church life, for the Church Record of the Warboys congregation has the following entry for the year 1655: 'The order of love-feast agreed upon, to be before the Lord's Supper; because the ancient churches did practise it, and for unity, with other churches near to us.' [2]

Another ordinance, exclusive to the Baptists, was that of Feet-washing. Their warrant for it was our Lord's humility in performing this menial service for his disciples, as recorded in the Fourth Gospel. It was, however, not generally insisted upon, as the Assembly of the General Baptists 'had long agreed that the practice of washing the feet of the saints, urged in Lincolnshire by Robert Wright in 1653, and in Kent by William Jeffrey in 1659, should be left optional as not specified in Hebrews vi'.[3]

The Baptists were as zealous as other Separatists in the exercise of ecclesiastical discipline; Helwys's church proceeded to the 'censures' every Sunday afternoon at the completion of the day's worship. Following the other Separatists they adopted a church covenant as the basis of the membership of the church, though there was some opposition amongst them to this procedure.

[1] Burrage, id., II, 106.
[2] Fenstanton, Warboys, and Hexham Records, ed. Underhill (1854), p. 272.
[3] Transactions of the Baptist Historical Society, I, p. 129 ff.

Hanserd Knollys, a leading Baptist minister, challenged anyone to demonstrate that the covenant had a basis in Scripture, nevertheless many Baptist churches were founded on covenants, notably Bunyan's church in Hitchin.

The peculiar contributions rendered by the Baptists to the worship and life of the English Separatists were three. They practised believers' baptism by immersion, thus retaining the Pauline symbolism of dying to sin, and being raised by faith in Christ. In the second place, they went further than the other Separatists in their opposition to forms of prayer, and in their esteem of spontaneity in worship. The third influence exerted by the Baptists was to become a regular feature of Puritan worship. This was the practice of running exposition or interpolated comment during public reading of the Scriptures. This was the custom of the old General Baptists, as Grantham's survey of their church life in 1678 clearly demonstrates, and it was indubitably employed by the New England Puritans. The originator was the distinguished English Baptist John Smyth.[1]

There are evidences of the existence of other Separatist congregations, but they cannot easily be affiliated to the three distinct groups enumerated above. There was a 'Privye Churche' that met in London in Queen Mary's time; its liturgy was the Edwardian Second Prayer Book. Its importance lies in the fact that it organized worship under persecution, and provided Elizabethan Separatists with a precedent for gathering secretly to worship in defiance of the laws of the realm, and in accordance with their own consciences. Another secret Church met at Plumbers Hall in 1567, but this

[1] *Works*, I, lxxxvii f.

may be regarded as the progenitor of the Presbyterian movement, since it used John Knox's Genevan Service Book. A similar congregation, also known as the 'Privye Churche', meeting under the leadership of Richard Fitz, was also discovered by the London authorities in 1567. Their adoption of a covenant makes it possible that they were the progenitors of Congregationalism. Their minister makes the three cardinal Puritan demands, declaring that the 'trewe markes of Christs churche' consist of :

Fyrste and formoste, the Glorious worde and Evangell preached, not in bondage and subjection, but freely, and purely. Secondly to have the Sacraments mynistred purely, onely and all together accordinge to the institution and good worde of the Lord Jesus, without any tradicion or invention of man. And laste of all, to have, not the fylthye Cannon Lawe, but dissiplyne onelye, and all together agreeable to the same heavenlye and almighty worde of our good Lorde, Jesus Chryste.[1]

The discipline so strongly insisted upon was practised at a special meeting convened on the fourth day of the week. The importance of the universal custom of ecclesiastical discipline amongst both Separatists and Puritans was its recognition that the churches of God are in need of a perpetual reformation.

The other feature of church life in which Separatists and Puritans shared was the use of a covenant. The fullest and most vivid description of the foundation of a church by covenant is that of the first Independent or Congregational church founded in London in 1616 by Henry Jacob.[2] A more elaborate covenant, almost,

[1] Peel, *The First Congregational Churches*, p. 32.
[2] For fuller details see pp. 56–7 *infra*.

in its solemnity and impressiveness, was that used by the Bassington Congregational Church which proceeds:

We do in the presence of the Lord Jesus the awful crowned King of Sion and in the presence of His holy angels, and people, and all beside here Solemnly give up ourselves to the Lord and to one another by the will of God, solemnly promising & engaging in the aforesaid presence to walk with the Lord, and with one another in the observation of all Gospel Ordinances and the discharge of all relative duties in this Church of God, & Elsewhere as the Lord shall enlighten and enable us.[1]

The outstanding importance of the covenant-relationship was twofold: it characterized Separatist and Puritan religion as an engagement of the heart in the service of Christ and His Church, as distinguished from a Creed stating the faith in intellectual propositions; in the second place, the contract as the basis of church relationships assumed an equality amongst the church members. In addition, since membership of the Church was by a voluntary covenant, it minimized the possibility of a merely nominal attachment to the Christian community.

Both Separatists and Puritans aimed at a 'further reformation according to the Word of God'. The only real difference between the two groups was that the former judged schism not too great a price to pay for immediate Reformation, whilst the latter sought constitutional means of attaining Reformation. Nevertheless, the Separatists had a profound influence on the Puritans in providing them with specific examples of liturgical experiments which gave concreteness to their theoretical considerations.

A second influence of the Separatists lay in their

[1] Burrage, *The Church Covenant Idea* (1904), p. 126.

radical opposition to set or 'stinted' forms of prayer. It
is true that free or extemporary prayer came to be the
distinctive contribution of the Free Churches to Christian worship; nevertheless it was a departure from
earlier Puritan tradition and from the liturgical practice
of the Continental Reformed Churches. Calvin prepared set liturgies for the worship of the cities of Strasbourg and Geneva; the English Presbyterians followed
the tradition in the Waldegrave Prayer Book.[1] Indeed,
as late as 1661, a leading Presbyterian, Richard Baxter,
compiled the Savoy Liturgy in the hope that this
formulary would prove acceptable both to the Anglican
and Reformed Communions in England. This tradition was deliberately set aside by the majority of English
Puritans. It is partly true that the imposition of successive revisions of the Book of Common Prayer bred in
the Puritans a distrust of all formularies of prayer. It
is equally true that the Separatists were the first to
urge that a form of prayer was a limitation of the operation of the Holy Spirit. It was due to them that John
Cotton, an Independent Puritan of the seventeenth
century, pleads the celebrated example of Tertullian
for *extempore* prayer, alleging that the early Christians
'prayed *sine monitore quia de pectore*, without a
prompter because they prayed from the heart'.[2] The
anonymous Puritan who wrote the *Anatomy of the
Service Book* is their debtor when he claims of the Book
of Common Prayer

... but this Booke settles such blinde fellows over
people, who can neither feed nor leade. What, we pray
you, is the procreant and conservant cause of dumb dogs

[1] See chapter III, p. 49 below.
[2] Cotton, *The Way of the Churches of Christ in New England*
(1645), p. 75.

that cannot barke; idle Shepheards, saying Sir Johns; meere Surplice and Service-book men, such as cannot doe so much as a Porter in his frocke; for he doth Service, and the Priest only sayes Service: is it not the Service-Book? [1]

In the course of time the Puritans came to join the Separatists. Doctrinally there was little to divide them, for they both believed that the Bible is the rule for faith and practice. The Puritans recollected that within the sixteenth century the worship, the doctrine, and the government of the English Church had been radically altered four times by the action of the sovereign and Parliament. *Prima facie* there was no reason why, with the growth of Puritan sentiment within the Establishment, there should not be a further legislative alteration. Rejected by Elizabeth, they hopefully approached James at the Hampton Court Conference, again to be disappointed. When the new claims of the Establishment as the guardian of episcopacy, *iure divino*, were heard in the mouths of the royal favourites, Bancroft and Laud, the hitherto patient and conforming Puritans began to lose their confidence in a constitutional change. Their only recourse now was to emigrate to New England, following in the wake of the Puritan Fathers, or to assist in the overthrow of a tyrannical and persecuting régime. Schism, before believed to be unthinkable, was now in the third decade of the seventeenth century seen to be inevitable. On this decision the Puritans and Separatists shook hands.

[1] *op. cit.* (1641), p. 47.

CHAPTER III

PRESBYTERIANS, CONGREGATION-ALISTS, AND BAPTISTS

OF the four leading Free Churches three are indigenous products of the English religious scene; namely, the Congregationalists, the Baptists, and the Methodists. Whilst Presbyterianism in England is a Swiss importation, by way of Scotland, it is significant that the first Presbytery was established at Wandsworth when Elizabeth was Queen. Presbyterianism was sponsored by the conforming Puritans, who complained of the inconsistency of the Queen in allowing refugees from Catholic persecution to celebrate worship according to the Reformed rites in the *ecclesia peregrinorum* in Canterbury, and in permitting the establishment of Presbyterianism in the Channel Islands, whilst she discouraged English Presbyterianism. The 'head' of the English Presbyterians, according to Fuller, was Thomas Cartwright. He was appointed Professor of Divinity in the University of Cambridge at the age of thirty-four. He celebrated this appointment by a series of inaugural lectures on the first two chapters of the Acts of the Apostles, pointing the contrast between the simplicity and spirituality of the Apostolic Church and the hierarchical and worldly character of the Elizabethan Church. This began a long theological feud between Cartwright and Whitgift, then Master of Trinity and the Archbishop of Canterbury of the future.

Cartwright's views at this time are summed up in *Six Articles*. The first demanded that the names and

D

functions of archbishops and archdeacons should be
abolished; the second, that the offices of lawful ministers
such as bishops and deacons, which were sanctioned by
the Scriptures, should be recalled to their apostolic
usage, with the bishop engaged in the ministry of the
Word and in prayer, and the deacon caring for the poor.
Thirdly, the government of each church should be in
the hands of its own minister and presbytery, or board
of elders, and not in the control of bishops, chancellors,
or archidiaconal officials. Further, each minister should
be in charge of some particular flock, and should not be
licensed to rove at large. In the fifth place, no man
should seek ministerial office by solicitation, as a gift
from a patron. Finally, ministers should be appointed
neither on the sole authority of bishops nor privately,
but by the election of the Church. These reforms,
urged Cartwright, should be implemented by the joint
action of magistrates, ministers, and laymen. As a
result of this open attack on the Establishment and on
the royal supremacy, Whitgift was able to procure
Cartwright's expulsion from Cambridge. He thought
it wise to leave the country, and ministered for twelve
years to the English merchants in Antwerp, and for a
further three years to an English congregation in
Middelburg. The assistance he thereafter gave to the
Presbyterian party in England was largely of a literary
nature. Nevertheless, although the planter of Presbyterianism in England was absent, the seed was growing
rapidly in secret.

It is possible to distinguish three stages in the
development of Presbyterian strategy under Elizabeth.
During the first decade of her reign they confined their
efforts to an attempt to purge the ecclesiastical trunk of
what they regarded as Roman Catholic fungus. As the

previous chapter indicated, their chief concern was to proscribe the Roman vestments and 'noxious cere-monies'. Their failure to achieve even these reforms forced them to delve more deeply into the fundamentals of 'Reformation according to the Word of God'. The second stage covers the years from 1572 to 1583, when their chief object was the formulation and propagation of Presbyterian principles. This period commenced with the *Order of Wandsworth* and concluded with the discovery by the High Commission of Cartwright's *Directory* in 1583. The third stage of development was the attempt to organize upon Presbyterian principles and to establish an *ecclesiola in ecclesia*, a Presbyterian society within the Established Church. Moreover, it was a time of vehement opposition, leading to the arrest and silencing of Cartwright and other leaders in the last decade of the century.

Our story has already taken us to the beginning of the second stage of development. The most vigorous statement of Presbyterian propaganda in this decade came from the pen of Cartwright, and was entitled the *Second Admonition*, following hard upon the heels of the *Admonition to Parliament* produced by Field and Wilcox. Cartwright broke a lance with Whitgift on two major issues: first, the scriptural constitution of the Church, and secondly, the abuses and corruptions re-maining within the Church of England. Whitgift maintained the sufficiency of Scripture as a rule for doctrine and behaviour, but denied that it was author-itative for worship and government. Cartwright upheld the sole sufficiency of Scripture for all necessary ecclesi-astical policy. Drysdale's comment on this point is judicious: 'If Cartwright went too far in insisting that the New Testament contains in express terms the exact

features of every true church, it is easy to see that
Whitgift's position essentially and logically involves the
Papacy and all its claims.'[1] Cartwright was ready to
recognize the royal supremacy over all cases civil and
ecclesiastical, but he claimed that there were spiritual
functions and jurisdictions belonging of right to the
office-bearers of the Church. If the power of the sword
belonged exclusively to the magistrate, the power of the
keys belonged exclusively to the Church and her rulers.
He contended that the right to proclaim the Gospel and
to exercise discipline on church members was a spiritual
function reserved for professedly spiritual persons.

The same decade is also remarkable for various
Presbyterian experiments that were attempted within
the framework of the Establishment, known respectively as the 'Discipline' and 'Prophesyings'. The
former was the inauguration of the Presbyterian form
of polity, and the latter were conferences of ministers
and devout laymen within a given district who gathered
to hear the exposition of the Word of God. Out of the
'Discipline' there grew the congregational eldership or
parochial presbytery; out of the 'Prophesyings' arose
the *Classis* or district presbytery.

In 1571 the town of Northampton was trying both
these experiments. On Sundays and holy days the
usual services according to the Prayer Book were followed, but various additions were made by zealous
ministers. A sermon was preached at Mattins, and on
Sunday afternoons the youth of the town were instructed
out of Calvin's *Catechism*. On Tuesdays and Thurs-
days, after an abbreviated service, there was a general
meeting of the congregation, with the mayor presiding,

[1] A. H. Drysdale, *History of the Presbyterians in England*
(1889), p. 155.

convened for spiritual discipline and the correction of evil-doers. There was also a meeting (for 'Prophesying') at which ministers might compare their doctrinal expositions and seek common light on obscure texts of Scripture. In addition, ministers of the county foregathered at a quarterly meeting to survey their performance of their tasks. Finally, a quarterly communion-service was celebrated. In each 'prophesying' three ministers were to expound the Scriptures, beginning with a simple elucidation of the passage, followed by the confutation of erroneous interpretations, and concluding with a practical application. The first speaker was allowed forty-five minutes for his discourse; the two subsequent speakers were limited to fifteen minutes each, in which time they had to make relevant additions, or correct any false interpretations. Each speaker began and ended with prayer and the whole exercise was completed within two hours. At the conclusion the leading preacher for the next exercise was appointed and a text given for his discourse. These arrangements were not substitutionary to, but supplementary to, the regular and normal ministrations of the Establishment, and those who attended, being the most devout, constituted a saving remnant within the wider Israel of the Church of England.

The paucity of preachers in England at that time was appalling. There was no preacher in all Cornwall, and only two in the diocese of Bangor. Bishop Sandys of Worcester told the Queen: 'Many there are that hear not a sermon in seven years, I might say in seventeen.'[1] In these circumstances the 'prophesyings' supplied a deeply felt need, and constituted miniature theological seminaries in which the Christian faith was expounded

[1] Drysdale, *op. cit.*, p. 127.

with clarity and orthodoxy. At the same, it presented
the Presbyterians with an opportunity, and they were
not slow to avail themselves of so advantageous a platform for the spread of their tenets.

The next year saw the establishment of the first
parochial presbytery in England. Eleven elders were
appointed at Wandsworth to co-operate with John
Field, the Lecturer at the parish church, in matters of
church rule and discipline amongst the Puritan portion
of the congregation. This, it is clear, was not the establishment of the full Presbyterian system, since no other
congregations were involved in the scheme, which did
not envisage setting up a classical or district presbytery.
Nevertheless, the decision to form a church session, as
it would be termed to-day, was not taken on the sole
responsibility of Field, for it was approved by an
association of Puritan ministers in London. The purpose of the institution was to maintain the purity
of communicants within the Church. The example
of Wandsworth was to be followed in hundreds of
churches throughout the land. This was only possible
because it involved no direct breakaway from the
Church of England.

A third event was to raise the hopes of the Presbyterian party for the future. That was the establishment
of Presbyterianism in the Channel Isles in 1576, under
the direction of the exiled Cartwright, and with the
reluctant permission of the Queen. Elsewhere Presbyterianism existed only in theory; here in reality, and as
a complete system. This miniature Geneva on English-
owned soil provided the model for the future. Here the
full Presbyterian form of church government had been
instituted, with the fourfold order of pastors, doctors
(or teachers), elders, and deacons. The pastor preached,

the doctor catechized, the elders supervised the conduct of members, and the deacons held and disposed of church properties and charities. There were three church courts: the consistory or local session, the presbytery, which met quarterly, and the synod, which was convened at two-yearly intervals. Provision was made for two services to be held each Lord's Day, and for a weeknight service. The worshippers joined in the Psalms and knelt for prayer, but, in fidelity to John Knox's 'black rubric', sat for the reception of the consecrated elements in the Lord's Supper, which was celebrated quarterly. Candidates for church membership were prepared and carefully examined on their knowledge of the faith by the pastors, and were scrutinized by the consistory. Sentences of excommunication were reserved for the supreme court of the Church, the synod, to pronounce. All these features of Church life in the Channel Islands were still pious dreams for their brethren in England.

None the less, it seemed that, with the success of the discipline and the prophesyings, Presbyterianism in England was gaining ground. But it was hardly more than a lusty infant when the Queen and her ecclesiastical advisers tried to strangle it. First the prophesyings were ruthlessly suppressed, despite the strenuous opposition of Archbishop Grindal and several of the bishops. The persecution of Presbyterians became more severe when Whitgift succeeded Grindal, and in 1583 he required subscription to fifteen further articles, including the sixth which affirmed that the Book of Common Prayer 'containeth in it nothing contrary to the Word of God'. Further, in the same year the Queen appointed forty-four High Commissioners to execute her ecclesiastical commands.

Both Puritans and Separatists suffered heavy reverses. Cartwright was imprisoned in 1585, and Robert Browne suffered a similar indignity for his convictions of the necessity of 'Reformation without tarrying for anie'. Both Cartwright and Browne were later to conform to the requirements of the Established Church, Cartwright accepting the Mastership of the Warwick Hospital, and Browne becoming Rector of Achurch-cum-Thorpe. Other leading Separatists, such as Barrowe, Greenwood, and Penry, were to pay for their beliefs with their life-blood. In 1593 Parliament tried a last desperate measure for suffocating dissent, passing *An Act to retain the Queen's Majesty's Servants in due obedience*. It was directed against those who denied, or tried to persuade others to reject, the Queen's supremacy in ecclesiastical affairs, or who attended unlawful religious assemblies. Suspects were to be committed to prison without bail and, if they did not recant within three months, they were to be banished from the realm. If they failed to leave, or returned without permission, they were to be hanged as felons.

How did the Presbyterians meet this hard blow? Some, despairing of constitutional change in ecclesiastical policy, became Separatists and sought asylum in Holland or Switzerland. Others conformed in the hope of a change of pilot at the government helm, and, cultivating Reformed doctrine and piety, were renowned as the 'doctrinal' Puritans of the succeeding reign. Such men were Rainolds, Perkins, Bolton, Preston, and the monumental Sibbes. Some were appointed as Lecturers in various townships; others accepted private chaplaincies in the houses of families of rank; others, again, accepted livings which were conveniently exempt from episcopal jurisdiction.

Elizabethan Presbyterianism was characterized by a high concern for preaching and for the purity of the Church. The form of church polity was designed to promote both these ends: for the pastor and teacher preached and taught the Biblical revelation, and the elders supervised discipline. Their form of worship rejected the sign of the cross in baptism, the ring in marriage, and kneeling for the reception of communion (the latter because it might countenance transubstantiation). The minister refused to wear the surplice and cope, as 'badges of Antichrist', preferring the grave, black, Genevan gowns. Presbyterians had no objection to a set liturgy, only to the particular liturgy of the Church of England then in vogue. In fact, the Presbyterians produced an English adaptation of Calvin's Genevan Form of Service, now known as the Waldegrave Liturgy, during Elizabeth's reign.[1] It has three Calvinistic characteristics: it is Biblical, didactic, and congregational. If the Presbyterian divines in the Westminster Assembly produced a *Directory* rather than a liturgy, it can only be because they were aware of the dangers of imposition and of the advantages of spontaneity and flexibility which the extemporary prayers expressed. The fuller establishment of Presbyterianism in England had to await the days of the Commonwealth and Protectorate.

If the Presbyterians were recruited from the conforming Puritans, the founders of the Congregationalists and Baptists were the non-conforming Puritans, or Separatists. They are distinguished from Presbyterians by their conception of the 'gathered church'.

[1] See the present writer's *The Worship of the English Puritans* (1948), pp. 122-7.

Whilst for Anglicans and Presbyterians in Elizabethan days a Christian nation and a Christian Church were co-extensive terms, for the Separatists and their followers a church consisted only of those gathered by God out of an unbelieving world.

An essential distinction between the Separatists and the Church of England was that between the 'sect' and the 'church' type of religious organization.[1] Congregationalists and Baptists disliked the view that all baptized persons in a parish were *eo ipso* members of the Church. They maintained, by contrast, that the Church should consist only of men and women who had consciously dedicated themselves to Christ and His service. Their importance lies in the extreme seriousness of their conception of church membership, which made hypocrisy and nominalism the chief enemies of the Christian community's reputation in the world.

That both denominations developed an independent and autonomous church polity was a direct consequence of their conception of the 'gathered Church'. For the Church could only remain pure if it were freed from the trammels of the hierarchy, whether civil or ecclesiastical. Their conviction was that the Church must be free from outside interference to offer complete surrender to Christ as King and Head.

Two further consequences followed from their independent church structures: in the first place the local congregation expressed fully the priesthood of all believers by appointing church officers from its midst, and by giving every member the privilege and responsibility of church government. In the second place, they recognized the folly of government coercion in spiritual

---

[1] A distinction first made by E. Troeltsch in *The Social Teaching of the Christian Churches.*

affairs, and it is not surprising that one of these denominations, the Baptists, nurtured the first apostles of
religious toleration in England.

As the Baptists originated in a secession from the Congregationalists, whose ecclesiastical polity they share, it
seems logical to outline the principles and polity of Congregationalism first. According to R. W. Dale, the first
Congregational church was that 'privye Church' in
London of which Richard Fitz was minister in 1567.[1]
Whether that was more Congregationalist than Presbyterian cannot be easily determined from the scanty
evidence extant. Again, in the case of the other Separatists, Greenwood, Barrowe, and Penry, one wonders
whether the church they attended in Southwark was
autonomous and independent by conviction, or by
necessity because it was clandestine. Would they, in
other words, have joined openly with other fellowships,
had the times been more propitious?

There is no doubt, however, that the first literary
exponent of Congregationalism was Robert Browne.
He was an impatient Puritan, who, opposing Cartwright's view, 'judged that the Kingdom of God was
not to be begun by whole parishes, but rather of the
worthiest, were they never so few'.[2] His principal
work on Congregationalism, printed at Middelburg in
Holland, was entitled *A Booke which sheweth the life and
manners of all true Christians*, and constituted a manual
of theology, ethics, and ecclesiology. His ecclesiology,
of primary relevance here, can be illustrated by excerpts.
He writes: 'the Church Government is the Lordship of
Christ in the communion of his offices: whereby his
people obey to his will, and have mutual use of their

[1] *History of English Congregationalism* (1907), p. 92 f.
[2] *A True and short Declaration . . .*, p. 6.

graces and callings, to further their godliness and welfare'.[1]

His polity clearly expresses the principle of the priesthood of all believers:

the *Kingdom* of all *Christians* is their office of their guiding and ruling with Christ, to subdue the wicked and make one another obedient to Christ. Their *priesthood* is their office of cleansing and redressing wickedness, whereby sin and uncleanness is taken away from amongst them . . . Their *prophecy* is their office of judging all things by the Word of God, whereby they increase in knowledge and wisdom among themselves.[2]

It is of the utmost importance to recognize that Christocracy, not democracy, was Browne's chief concern. He had no intention of establishing a church order where *vox populi* should count as *vox Dei*; where churchmen could believe what they chose to, or act as they wished. He based the powers and responsibility of the Christian commonalty upon their union with Christ, whose regal, priestly, and prophetic offices they share.

Moreover, it is significant that Browne did not believe in the absolute autonomy and independence of the individual church. If a particular church could not clearly discern the will of Christ in any question at issue, it was to invite other churches (as churches, not by means of representatives) to confer with them and advise them. In addition, Browne did not hold that the elders of a church received authority from the people: on the contrary, he taught that pastor, teacher, and elder have 'office and message of God'. The task of the church was merely to recognize those to whom such gifts had been granted by God.

Browne's life is of little importance, because he later

[1] *op. cit.*, 35.   [2] *op. cit.*, 55.

conformed, but his ideas were to fructify in Congregationalism as a form of church polity. The early Separatists were to die as martyrs for the cause that Browne relinquished. They were to depart from the Genevan tradition in recognizing not merely the inadequacy of the Anglican liturgy, but the insufficiency of all liturgies. One of the most cultured of them, Henry Barrowe, made the most eloquent plea for free prayer as against fixed forms:

Shall we think that God hath at any time left these his servants so singly furnished and destitute of his grace, that they cannot find words according to their necessities, and faith to express their wants and desires, but need thus to be taught line unto line, as children newly weaned from the breasts, what and when to say, and when to make an end? Prayer I take to be a confident demanding through the Holy Ghost, according to the will of God. . . .[1]

This tradition of free prayer was to live on in Congregationalism throughout the centuries. The Separatists also gave Congregationalism two other gifts; a covenant-relationship as the basis of the gathered church, in which the members pledged themselves to serve God and each other in His ordinances, and a democratic form of church order, in which all the members shared. This was a priceless heritage. It is even possible that the secret church in London, to which the three martyrs Barrowe, Greenwood, and Penry belonged, was the first English Congregational church.

On their deaths, the other members of the secret London congregation crossed into Holland, where we must look for the further development of Congregationalism. Francis Johnson, their pastor, followed them

[1] *A Brief Discoverie of the False Church*, pp. 64-5.

to Amsterdam, where he ministered to a congregation of three hundred exiles. The teacher of the church was that renowned Hebraist, Henry Ainsworth. The officers of the church also included four ruling elders, three deacons, and one deaconess. The latter appointment is an example which the other Free Churches took almost three centuries to imitate.

Meanwhile, there was in the early days of James I's reign a renaissance of Congregationalism in England, on the borders of Yorkshire, Nottinghamshire, and Lincolnshire. Its leader was John Smyth of Gainsborough, a former Puritan minister and Fellow of Christ's College, Cambridge. In 1604 John Robinson, a former Fellow of Corpus Christi in the same university, joined this church. The ruling elder of the congregation was William Brewster, later to become famous as the leader of the Pilgrim Fathers who sailed for New England aboard the *Mayflower* in 1620. Other members of this distinguished conventicle were Helwys and Murton, later to found the first General (or Arminian) Baptist church in England at Newgate, and Bradford, the future governor of New Plymouth.

For convenience the church was divided into two congregations, and those living nearer to Scrooby detached themselves from the Gainsborough fellowship. At Scrooby, Richard Clyfton became pastor, John Robinson teacher, and William Brewster the ruling elder. In 1606 the Gainsborough members emigrated to Amsterdam, where the Scrooby congregation soon followed them. Smyth and the Gainsborough church joined the congregation of London exiles in Amsterdam, but Robinson, learning of the dissensions within this community, thought it wiser to move on to Leyden with his flock.

In Amsterdam Smyth was advancing heterodox views, believing in a purely pneumatic worship which despised English translations of the Scriptures and Psalm-books. As a result, he and most of his people withdrew to form a second Congregational church in Amsterdam. Ultimately he became dissatisfied with infant Baptism, and baptized himself and his congregation. Thus he formed the first English Baptist congregation. Meanwhile, Johnson in the other church was claiming almost tyrannical and inquisitorial powers for the eldership over the commonalty of the church. Ainsworth, pleading the priesthood of all believers, disagreed, and withdrew, accompanied by thirty associates, to form the third Congregational church in Amsterdam.

Robinson's church in Leyden consisted of peaceable people, but they felt they could not indefinitely remain in friendly exile. Many reasons urged them to emigrate to Virginia. They were afraid that their children would become Dutch. They were perturbed at the slack observance of the Lord's Day on the part of their Dutch neighbours. Their children, becoming impatient of the hard life, went to sea or joined the army and succumbed to the great temptations of these avocations. Their monies were almost spent, and they had either to live meanly or return to England. Finally, they were eager to advance the spread of the Gospel in the remote parts of the earth under the English flag.

In 1620 the church gathered to bid farewell to those determined to make the great adventure. There John Robinson made a famous oration, remarkable for the forward look of its theology and for its irenical temper, in which the genius of Congregationalism found fit expression. He said:

I charge you, before God and His blessed angels, that you follow me no further than you have seen me follow the Lord Jesus Christ. If God reveal anything to you by any other instrument of His, be as ready to receive it as you were to receive any truth by my ministry, for I am verily persuaded the Lord hath more truth yet to break forth out of His holy word. For my part I cannot sufficiently bewail the condition of those Reformed Churches which are come to a period in religion and will go at present no further than the instruments of their reformation. The Lutherans cannot be drawn to go beyond what Luther saw. Whatever part of His will our God has revealed to Calvin, they will die rather than embrace; and the Calvinists, you see, stick fast where they were left by that great man of God, who yet saw not all things. That is a misery much to be lamented.[1]

The company left in the *Speedwell*, which was found unseaworthy at Land's End, and they continued their journey from Plymouth in the *Mayflower*, to establish a denomination in New England which in 1949 numbered 1,173,626 members,[2] and an *entente cordiale* between the two great English-speaking nations, which has endured even the tensions of the American War of Independence and two world conflicts.

It was Henry Jacob, a member of Robinson's Leyden church, who was to re-establish Congregationalism in England. A former Puritan, he had associated himself with Robinson because he approved of the latter's critical but charitable recognition of congregations within the Establishment as true Christian churches. In 1616 he founded the first Congregational church to

[1] Indirect speech in E. Winslow, *Hypocrisie Unmasked*, pp. 97–8; direct speech as given in Skeats and Miall, *History of the Free Churches of England*, (1891), p. 34.
[2] A. Peel and D. Horton, *International Congregationalism* (1949), p. 88.

remain in continuous existence at Southwark. It was inaugurated on the simple basis of a covenant bond:

> Each of the brethren made open confession of his faith in our Lord Jesus Christ; and then, standing together, they joined hands and solemnly covenanted with each other in the presence of Almighty God, to walk together in all God's ways and ordinances, according as He had revealed, or should further make known to them. Mr. Jacob was then chosen pastor by the suffrage of the brotherhood, and others were appointed to the office of deacons, with fasting and prayer and imposition of hands.[1]

The pastor was the sole elder, and the other officers were deacons. Thus the fourfold order of Leyden and Amsterdam was attenuated to a twofold order. Jacob combined the preaching and teaching offices, and the deacons shared in the spiritual oversight of the church with the pastor, in addition to controlling the finances of the congregation. This form of church polity has become characteristic and almost invariable within Congregational churches subsequently founded.

The distinctive features of Congregational worship were three: rejecting a liturgy, they used only extemporary prayers; they celebrated the Lord's Supper on every Lord's Day, and not quarterly, as did the Presbyterians: and their communion order was characterized by a double consecration, that is, a separate consecration of the bread and of the wine.

Their chief contribution to the Universal Church was the conception of the priesthood of all believers, as written into the constitution of the Church: a principle which was to produce, as a by-product, stalwart

[1] Hanbury, *Historical Memorials* (1841), I, p. 292 f.

E

defenders of democratic rights in the constitutional struggle against Stuart absolutism. A second contribution of great significance was their choice of a covenant to replace a creed, due to their recognition that the devotion of the heart is deeper than the assent of the intellect.

It cannot now be determined how much the Baptists owed to the Continental Anabaptists, and how much to English Congregationalists, for their foundation.[1] Certainly the first Baptists found it embarrassing to be associated with the millenarian fanatics of Münster. Nevertheless they had affinities with the Anabaptists. The latter were distinguished by nine characteristics. (i) They insisted that a church should consist only of converted Christians. (ii) They rebaptized all who joined them and had been baptized in infancy—hence they were called Anabaptists, or Rebaptizers. (iii) They rejected infant baptism. (iv) They called themselves 'brethren', or 'disciples'. (v) They taught that unbaptized infants were saved, and (vi) that the Lord's Supper was a badge of faith. (vii) They practised feet-washing as a dominical ordinance, and (viii) expressed in their constitution the priesthood of all believers. (ix) Biblically and socially they were radicals, denying the State's right to compel belief, refusing to take civil oaths or to bear arms, and being opposed to lending out money for interest. Some of them practised a Christian communism. Most of these characteristics were shared by the English Baptists.

[1] The reader should consult P. T. Forsyth's *Faith, Freedom and the Future* for a detailed appreciation of the debt which the Calvinistic Free Churches (Baptist and Congregationalist) owe to the Anabaptists of the Continent for the formulation of their ecclesiologies.

The first English Baptist, John Smyth, however, appears to have had no connexion with the Anabaptists until after he had reached the Baptist position. Beginning as a clergyman in the Church of England, he became a Congregationalist, and finally a Baptist. As a member of the Gainsborough church which emigrated to Amsterdam in 1608, Smyth soon became engaged in controversy with Francis Johnson, the minister of the Congregational church in the city of exiles. He held that in reading the Scriptures a translation should be made direct from the Hebrew and Greek, and he objected to sermons being read and psalms being sung from a book. He was before his time in declaring that a collection was an act of worship, and should be hallowed by prayer. He declared that the New Testament knew of only two orders of ecclesiastical officers: bishops, also called elders or presbyters, and deacons, who were to be received by the election, approbation, and ordination of the local church. Endeavouring to constitute his church entirely upon New Testament foundations, he became convinced that the apostolic method of admitting members to church fellowship was by baptism on profession of repentance towards God and faith in Christ.

He then drew the inference that the baptism he and his congregation had received in the English parish churches was invalid. They must, therefore, reconstitute the Church not on a basis of mutual covenant, but by the baptism of all professed believers. Smyth proceeded first to baptize himself, then Thomas Helwys, and finally the rest. Thus in 1609 was founded the first English Baptist church, though on Dutch soil. The method of baptism was not immersion, as might be expected, but affusion from a basin.

Smyth became dissatisfied not only with the paedo-baptism of the Congregationalists, but even with their theology. He became a convinced Arminian, believing that Christ died not only for the elect but for all mankind. As a consequence of this, he became a stout defender of the principle of religious toleration for all men. The first claim for full religious liberty ever penned in the English language was written by Smyth. It read:

[We believe] that the magistrate is not by virtue of his office to meddle with religion or matters of conscience, to force and compel men to this or that form of religion or doctrine: but to leave the Christian religion free to everyman's conscience, and to handle only civil transgressions, injuries, and wrongs of man against man, in murder, adultery, theft, etc., for Christ only is the King and Lawgiver of the Church and conscience.[1]

Smyth, therefore, is not only the first English apostle of religious toleration for all men, but the founder of the Baptists in England and of the General Baptists in particular.

His colleague, Thomas Helwys, returned to England in 1612, believing it to be cowardly to remain in exile while his comrades were suffering persecution. He founded the first Baptist church on English soil at Spitalfields, outside the walls of the City of London, in the same year. Like Smyth, Helwys stood for religious toleration and published his views in *A Short Declaration of the Mystery of Iniquity*. For this enlightened defence of religious liberty he was thrown into prison, where he died in 1616. The mantle of leadership now fell upon his colleague in exile, John Murton.

[1] Cited A. C. Underwood, *A History of the English Baptists* (1947), p. 42.

General Baptist churches increased in number despite persecution, and in 1626 there were congregations of this persuasion in Lincoln, Salisbury, Coventry, and Tiverton. The Congregationalists, at this time, were still imbued with the Calvinistic idea that it was the duty of civil powers to encourage true religion and suppress the false. The early General Baptists believed that no man was predestined by a divine decree to damnation, but that all men might repent and believe the Gospel, and that none were irretrievably lost. They drew the conclusion that to destroy a man for his mistaken beliefs might defeat the purpose of God for his salvation. Living, he might be reclaimed from the error of his ways, if the truth were presented to him without coercion. It was, therefore, no accident that the Arminian General Baptists were the first to plead for complete freedom of conscience for all.

The other branch of the English Baptists, the Particular or Calvinistic Baptists, also emerged as a secession from within Congregationalism. They were called 'Particular' because they believed in a particular or restricted atonement, confined to the elect. This branch of the Baptists was a secession from the Southwark Congregational church founded by Henry Jacob in 1616. It appears that in 1633 a certain Samuel Eaton and some other members of the church adopted the opinions of the appropriately named Mr. Dipper, who had left the church three years earlier, because they contested the validity of parish baptism. Whether they rejected infant baptism, as such, is not known. In 1638, however, there arises a group of six people who were convinced that baptism was not to be administered to infants, but only to convinced Christian adults. This group professed to be 'of the same judgment with Sam

Eaton'.[1] Having decided who were the proper subjects of baptism, there remained two other unresolved questions: namely, the proper mode of baptism, and the proper administrator of the ordinance. They solved the first problem by deciding on immersion, as consonant with the Pauline description of salvation as dying and rising again with Christ. On the second issue, they agreed that it was not essential for the administrator of baptism to have been himself baptized. Soon immersion was accepted as the recognized mode of baptism by all Baptist Churches, whether General or Particular.

Both these sections of the Baptist movement, probably because of their toleration and strong democratic views, came to exert a profound influence in the days of the Commonwealth. The more radical amongst them gravitated to the Fifth Monarchy milleniarists, and it is significant that it was a Baptist society at Mansfield which in 1648 'first supplied George Fox with congenial religious fellowship, and, under his leadership, developed into the earliest Quaker congregation'.[2] By 1640 the Baptists had seven congregations in London, and forty-seven in the rest of England. Three hundred years later, this indigenously English religious movement had developed into one of the largest Protestant associations of churches in the world, with a total membership of thirteen and a half million souls.[3]

[1] A. C. Underwood, *op. cit.*, p. 58.
[2] Braithwaite, *The Beginnings of Quakerism*, pp. 12 and 43.
[3] Grubb and Bingle (ed.), *World Christian Handbook* (World Dominion Press, 1949), p. 240.

CHAPTER IV

UNDER THE COMMONWEALTH
AND PROTECTORATE

WHILST it may be true that most religious crusades end in business arrangements, and that the Commonwealth degenerated into a Protectorate that seemed to be hardly distinguishable from a dictatorship, there can be no doubt that the driving force of the anti-monarchical armies was religious. There also seems to be little doubt that if the Roundheads had been more united religiously, the Restoration of the monarchy might have been indefinitely postponed. Indeed, it appears that it was the overweening disregard of liberties by Charles I and his advisers that fomented the Puritan reaction, and kept the Puritans united. When Charles and Laud were dead, the victors fell out. It is one of the ironies of history that a coalition of the Presbyterians and Erastian Anglicans established the Commonwealth, whilst the plea of the Independents and the parties to their left for toleration dissolved the Commonwealth to establish a greater liberty, producing such anarchy that Cromwell reluctantly assumed the office of Lord Protector to enforce law and order. Again, it was their common sufferings under the Clarendon Code that consolidated Presbyterians, Independents, and Baptists into a unity they had never known in the days of their triumph.

From the days that the hopes of the Puritans were dashed at the Hampton Conference by James's epigram 'No bishop, no king', there were two alternatives open to them. They could either, like Cordelia, 'sit and be silent', or emigrate. It has been estimated that over twenty thousand crossed the Atlantic to the new American colonies between 1620 and 1640, to find the religious freedom which England refused them. The lot of those who remained was, if anything, harder, for they had to submit to a despotism that grew increasingly intolerant. Even the compliant and moderate Anglicans became restive as the King asserted his divine right, and Archbishop Laud insisted upon the revival of Roman ceremonial. *The Book of Sports* issued by James I in 1618, and re-issued by Charles I in 1633, was the least of the Puritan vexations, but this struck at their conception of Sunday as the Lord's day. Even so moderate a man as Richard Baxter complains that the merriment interfered with the exercise of family worship in so small a village as Eaton Constantine: 'So that we could not read the Scripture in our family without the great disturbance of the tabor and pipe and noise in the street.' [1] Although, as a youth, his inclination was to join in the fun, he adds: 'when I heard them call my father Puritan it did much to cure me and alienate me from them; for I considered that my father's exercise of reading the Scripture was better than theirs, and would surely be better thought on by all men at the last . . .' [1] No opportunity was lost, it seems, for taunting men who made it their chief task to glorify God. Those ministers who conscientiously opposed the wearing of the surplice, the metamorphosis of the communion-table into an altar, the use of the sign of the cross at baptism, and kneeling for the reception of the holy communion, were treated like criminals. They were haled before the bishop or the Court of High

[1] *The Autobiography of Richard Baxter*, Everyman edn., p. 6.

Commission and were there ordered to be punished sometimes with a sadistic severity. While the Archbishop offended the consciences of the religious, the King, aided by Buckingham and Strafford, defied the constitutional rights of the people by dispensing with Parliament for eleven years. He went on to mulct the common man by rigorous taxation. The peak of insensitivity was reached when Laud, with the royal assent, attempted to impose upon the Scots a High-Church Prayer Book, which forced the Scottish Presbyterians into the Parliamentarian camp, and ultimately produced, by reaction, the Solemn League and Covenant. The revolt, long kindled privately, flared into public rebellion in the Civil Wars.

What then were the religious forces which the conjoint tyranny of Charles and Laud forced into cohesion? In general, they may be described as Puritans and Erastians. The Puritans consisted predominantly of Presbyterians (joined by Independents and other sects), whose aim was to reform England after the Genevan model and to establish presbyterian classes in the place of episcopal dioceses. They were united with the Erastian Low-Churchmen in believing that Charles and Laud were tyrants, and that both monarchy and episcopacy should be tamed by Parliament. Neither party, however, would have followed the Independents and the sects in their plea for religious toleration. In that sense, they were all Erastians. The Presbyterians hoped to see uniformity, but Presbyterian uniformity, insisted upon as the State-established Church, and made a strenuous attempt to achieve this result through the Westminster Assembly of Divines. With the Erastians, they were strong supporters of the sovereignty of Parliament, and their influence in the legislative body was strong. However, in time of war, Parliament requires as auxiliaries an army and a treasury. The City of London, the Parliamentary treasury, also strongly supported the Presbyterians, but their greatest weakness was ultimately to lie in the army itself, for it was there that the Independents and sects predominated. At first, as the soldiers received their payment regularly, the army was the obedient servant of the Presbyterian religious party, but when the City was bled white, and the army realized, with Milton, that 'new presbyter is but old priest writ large', both officers and men turned increasingly to the Independent party which promised toleration for all the variety of sects. To Milton, the Latin Secretary, and to Cromwell, the Protector, Independency offered the only hope of religious peace. The victors in the conflict between Parliament and King can, therefore, be subdivided into three groups (or, if the small but influential group of Erastians is included, into four groups). These were: the Presbyterians, the Independents, and the Sectaries. The last may, again, be further subdivided into two classes: the one class might be described as religious democrats, and comprised the Anabaptists and the Fifth Monarchy men, whilst the second class might be called the secular democrats, and this included the Diggers and Levellers. During the period of the Commonwealth, the Presbyterians and Erastians held the reins of power and almost succeeded in establishing Presbyterianism in England. During the period of the Protectorate, the Independents and the Sectaries shared power with Oliver, and it was at this time that there was no established or State Church in England, and the maximum of religious toleration was achieved.

The English Presbyterians in this grouping are

clearly to be distinguished from the Scottish Presbyterians, with whom they had no contact until 1643,
when the Scottish Commissioners travelled to London
to give effect to the implications of the Solemn League
and Covenant. It is clear from the debates of the
Westminster Assembly of Divines that the Scots
brethren believed in the divine right of presbytery,
whereas their English brethren placed the laity almost
on a parity with the ministry. In addition, the Presbyterian party in Parliament relied upon the support of
the Erastians; it was the right wing of the Puritan
coalition and agreed with the Erastians both in desiring
a State Church and in its conservative civil policy. In
contradistinction from the Independents and the democratic Sectaries, the Presbyterians wished to assert the
supremacy of Parliament, not of the people, and to
preserve the rights of property. They supported a
limited monarchy in the interests of a lasting peace.
Their policy, the revolutionary insistence on the
Genevan Church order excepted, appeared to be an
attempt to persuade the people of England that they
were not revolutionaries at all. In these circumstances,
it is not surprising either that the King chose to treat
with them, and, in refusing their terms, lost his crown
and his head, or that it was the Presbyterian party
which eventually ended the Protectorate and effected
the restoration of the monarchy.

The Independents rose to power on a wave of opposition to the clericalism of the Presbyterian party. They
were numerically small during the zenith of Presbyterian power, and rested content with a State-controlled
Presbyterianism, provided that toleration was afforded
to those of their way ecclesiastically. Their strength
consisted almost exclusively in their unmitigated plea

for toleration, which enabled them to count on the support of the parties of the left, who were unrepresented in the House of Commons. In time, as their strength in the army increased, and as 'new Parliament bore a striking resemblance to old king',[1] the rift between the Independents and the Presbyterians grew. So sensitive were they to parliamentary tyranny that they sought to limit the duration of Parliament, and, taking a leaf out of the book of their left-wing comrades, the Levellers, they proposed a biennial Parliament. Ultimately, losing faith in the existing Parliament, they agreed to Cromwell's suggestion that he and his Council should nominate a Parliament of godly men, which would contain a very high proportion of Independents. Happily, for them, the main tenets of the Independents had been formulated by the beginning of the fourth decade of the century, more particularly in a work by John Cotton, the New England pastor of Boston, entitled *The True Constitution of a Particular Visible Church*, published in 1642. This was clearly the foundation of the *Apologeticall Narration*, by which the Independent minority in the Westminster Assembly of Divines apprised the nation of its distinctive theological platform. They held that the Scriptures alone provided the sole standard and rule in all doctrinal and liturgical matters. For that reason they excluded from their worship all ecclesiastical actions devised by men, deriding customs for which they could find no warrant in Holy Writ as mere 'will-worship'. Their distinctive form of church government, which gave complete autonomy to the local church, making it 'independent' of State or hierarchical control, was based on the belief that every company or congregation of believers, joined

[1] A. S. P. Woodhouse, *Puritanism and Liberty*, p. 17.

together in the hearing of the Word and in the celebration of the two gospel sacraments, was a true, visible church of Jesus Christ. As a corollary, all churches and congregations are equal, and churches have the right to set apart and ordain their pastors, teachers, and ruling elders. They further held that ecclesiastical officers have no right to impose any physical or financial penalty on transgressors, and that the most a church can do, is to excommunicate an erring member. To these distinctively Independent doctrines, they added, as will be seen later in detail, a theory of toleration, holding that local churches and individual persons are free from political or ecclesiastical interference. This view was most radically expressed by John Goodwin, who proposed to extend liberty to Papists, Turks, and Jews.[1] Independency was important, according to Mr. David Ogg, because:

It was from Independency, not Presbyterianism, that English Puritanism was to draw its strength, for Presbyterianism was foreign and autocratic, while Independency was the reincarnation of the traditional discontent of the 'small man' anxious for the solace of a personal and intimate faith, and repelled by the spectacle of a wealthy, secular-minded Church.[2]

The same author adds that the Independents 'inherited something of the old Lollard antagonism to the earthly, arrogant church'. In view of this dual emphasis on criticism of political pretensions and the plea for toleration, it is not surprising that the Independents played an important mediating role in the Commonwealth, and the major role in the days of the Protectorate.

[1] *A Reply of two of the Brethren to A.S.*, pp. 55–6.
[2] In *Christianity in the Light of Modern Knowledge*, Pt. v, Chap. II, p. 662.

To the left of the Independents were the Sectaries, both religious and secular. The latter comprised such parties as the Levellers, and the even more radical Diggers, whose views are of no religious significance. Of the religious group the most significant were the Anabaptists (or Baptists), and the Fifth Monarchy men, many of whom seceded from the ranks of the Baptists. The Sectaries as a whole agreed with the Independents in stressing the autonomy of the local congregation and the necessity for toleration. This second tenet was, of course, the basis of their alliance with the Independent party. The religious sectarians were a seed-plot of democracy, because in their autonomous churches every member shared in the responsibility for ruling the affairs of the church, and had experienced the cut and thrust of ecclesiastical debate. It would not, however, be strictly accurate to describe either the Anabaptists, or the Fifth Monarchy men, as pure democrats, since they emphasized the rights of the saints rather than the privileges of the people, and looked forward to a Millennium in which saints should inherit the earth and rule it as the vicegerents of Christ. John Rogers, formerly a Presbyterian minister, may be taken as a typical exponent of Fifth Monarchy principles, with its eschatological expectations. In *Sagrir* published in 1653, he wrote:

✔ Schoolboys look after holidays: worldly men after rent days: chapmen after market days: travellers after fair days: professors after Lord's days: and the people of God after those days of Christ, viz. the end of the four monarchies, that the Fifth may come wherein Christ and his saints shall rule the world.

The 'four monarchies' referred to are the Assyrian, Persian, Macedonian, and Roman. Fifth Monarchy men were, in their way, theological levellers, for Rogers pleads for the abolition of clergy, tithes, and lawyers, and urges an aggressive foreign policy to unite all Protestants in the destruction of all 'Norman and Babylonian yokes'. The Putney Debates of the army make it clear that these views were held by many of the rank and file, while they were espoused by Colonels Harrison and Goffe.

It is doubtful whether the Baptists drank of such heady eschatological beverages, and their nearest allies were the Independents, whose structure of church order they copied. The Baptists, as has been said, comprised Particular and General: the former were Calvinists, who held firmly to the doctrine of election, whilst the latter had Arminian tendencies. On the whole, their ministers were not as well educated as the Independent ministry, probably because the other Protestant churches regarded them as heretics in their demand for adult baptism, and refused them access to the universities. One of their number was, however, a most learned and doughty controversialist, John Toombes, who took it upon himself to challenge the entire Assembly of Westminster Divines. There were seven Particular Baptists churches in London in 1643, which in that year published a Confession of Faith. Their influence spread during the Commonwealth, and particularly during the Protectorate, when their ministers collaborated with the Presbyterians and the Independents on the Committee of Triers. Their three representatives on that Committee were John Toombes, Jessey, and Dyke. In 1645 Hanserd Knollys founded a Baptist Church in Great St. Helens, London. Meanwhile, as dogmatic Calvinism weakened with the downfall of Presbyterianism, the General Baptists made headway, forming churches in Spalding, Hunstanton, and Warboys, while adding to their churches in Kent.[1] Perhaps their most notable lay leader was the courteous and accomplished Colonel Hutchinson. Their most notable contribution to the religion of the Commonwealth was a literary one, from the pen of a New England Baptist, Roger Williams, who was widely read in England. His influence was the greater because he lived in England from 1643 to 1644 and from 1651 to 1654. There had been before him several to plead for religious toleration on grounds of expediency, but his distinction lies in basing his appeal on the liberty of conscience. His greatest book, *The Bloody Tenent of Persecution*, was issued in 1644. He begins by interpreting the Parable of the Tares as a proof that magistrates are prohibited from using compulsion in the matters of faith. His plea for toleration extends to the Roman Catholics, who are battened under the hatches of the ship of State. He derides the notion that physical compulsion can either deter heretics from their heresies or create orthodox Christians. This was a warning which the belligerent ecclesiastical partisans of the seventeenth century would have done well to heed. For as Anglicans in power had persecuted Presbyterians, so Presbyterians in power dispossessed Anglicans. The most celebrated passage of the book is that in which Williams argues for the complete separation of Church and State. Christ, he claims, has appointed his ministers to be the unquestioned masters of the ship which is the Church. The pilot may not steer a false course, or change course, even at the behest of the prince, who

[1] Jordan, *The Development of Religious Toleration in England*, III, p. 457, estimates that there were 297 Baptist churches founded prior to 1660 in England and Wales.

is no more than a passenger in the ship whose sails
are set towards the attainment of divine truth. Should
the prince persist in his attempt to handle the ship to
the peril of its company, the crew may resist these
dangerous practices and so save the ship. In the same
way, the ship of State is governed absolutely by its
master, the magistrate, who steers it towards safety
and prosperity. He can tolerate no interference from
the members of the Church, his passengers, whilst
sailing his proper course.[1]

During the days of the Commonwealth, and precisely
at the time that Presbyterian dominance was at its
zenith, the most anti-authoritarian expression of religion, Quakerism, was also making headway. It was
in the year of the Westminster Assembly that George
Fox first experienced a spiritual unrest, and in 1646,
the year of the edict for the establishment of Presbyterianism, that he found peace. Tired of an autocratic church, dissatisfied with a Presbyterian autocracy,
sick of the bibliolatry of the Independents, and of the
general formalism and hypocrisy of contemporary religion, Fox found the inner authority and illumination
of the Holy Spirit. By this interior illumination and
peace, he was enabled to endure ridicule and ignominy,
persecution and imprisonment. In the early Commonwealth days of the Society of Friends, their eccentricity
rather than their sincerity impressed the minds of
his contemporaries. Some Quakers brought the name
into contempt by appearing naked in public. More
dangerous to the cause was the messianism of James
Nayler, a prominent Quaker, who rode in triumph to the
city of Bristol acclaimed by the hysterical hosannas of
his followers. The severity of the sufferings of the

[1] *op. cit.*, p. 378.

Quakers during a time of unexampled toleration must be ascribed to their refusal to take oaths in courts of law, or to doff their caps at the presence of authority. Their sincerity is, however, shown by the penalties they would pay rather than compromise their principles. It is computed that 3,173 Quakers were imprisoned during the Protectorate, and that thirty-two died in prison.[1] Cromwell, who chose to interview Fox himself, was greatly impressed by the religious insight of the Quaker leader. As Fox left his presence, the Protector said: 'Come again to my house. If you and I were but an hour a day together, we should be nearer to each other.'[2]

It was also during this period that Unitarianism first appeared in England. John Biddle, the father of English Socinianism, was tried by Cromwell's parliament. It is largely to Cromwell's credit that Biddle received every opportunity to clear himself, and that the more orthodox were restrained from giving vent to sadistic savagery in the treatment of the heretic.

The pulse of Presbyterian religious life may be felt in the Westminster Assembly of Divines, which was charged with the responsibility of advising Parliament on a religious settlement. This was a body of 162 clergy and laymen, which was named the Westminster Assembly because it met in Henry VII's Chapel during the summer and in the Jerusalem Chamber of the Abbey during the colder months. It consisted of 30 lay assessors of whom 10 were Lords and 20 Commoners;

[1] Skeats and Miall, *History of the Free Churches of England*, p. 55.
[2] Carlyle, *Cromwell's Letters and Speeches* (ed. Lomas), II, p. 464.

121 English Divines (of whom only 5 were Independents); 3 Scribes; and 8 Scottish Commissioners (of whom 5 were clerical and 3 lay members). It owed its existence to the Long Parliament's acceptance of the Solemn League and Covenant, involving the establishment of the National Church on Presbyterian lines as the price of Scottish military assistance. Whilst there was an overwhelming majority of Presbyterians, the Independents gave a good account of themselves, and proved to be a penetrating and constructive opposition. This minority comprised: Thomas Goodwin (later to become President of Magdalen College, Oxford), Nye, Burroughs, Bridge, Carter, Caryll, Phillips, and Sterry (a renowned mystic in Restoration days). Many of them were as learned as their opponents, and most of them were now tasting the precious fruits of religious freedom after exile in Holland, and were therefore as keen for liberty as for reform. The Presbyterians, however, were only interested in a reform of the Church after the Genevan manner.

The Assembly was charged with seven tasks: first, the revision of the Thirty-nine Articles of Religion; second, the establishment of a Presbyteral form of church government; third, the establishment of ecclesiastical discipline; fourth, making arrangements for regular ordinations of ministerial candidates; fifth, the production of a Directory of worship; sixth, the provision of a Confession of Faith; and, finally, the production of the Larger and Shorter Catechisms. In the first task the Assembly proceeded no further than to revise the first sixteen Articles, preferring ultimately to produce its own Confession of Faith. The second, its main task, was not satisfactorily executed, partly because of the virulence and persistence of the Independent opposition, partly because only in London and Essex was Presbyterianism popular, and other areas resisted the imposition of a presbyteral form of ecclesiastical government. The Assembly argued to no purpose on the next task, the establishment of ecclesiastical discipline, for the members could not agree on what sins were to be denominated scandalous, nor whether clergy or congregations were to exercise the right of excommunication. The members were, however, more successful in the production of their Confession of Faith, which was a clearly defined Calvinist creed, and the same unanimity characterized the composition of the Larger and the justly famous Shorter Catechism with its noble definition: 'Man's chief end is to glorify God, and to enjoy Him forever.' The Presbyterian proposals for ordination were nullified by Independent criticism.

So, apart from the Confessions and Catechisms, the chief contribution of the Westminster Assembly to English religious life was its *Directory for the Public Worship of God in the three Kingdoms*. Possibly its success is due to the fact that it was a *via media* between a prescribed liturgy and extemporaneous prayer. It is indisputable that it was to provide the norm of Presbyterian, Independent, and Baptist worship for almost three centuries, itself a great achievement. The preparation of a rough draft of the devotional manual was in the hands of a small sub-committee, consisting of Marshall, Palmer, Young, Herle, the Scottish Commissioners, and Goodwin, the Independent. In these circumstances there is little room for surprise that the resulting Directory should betray strong Scottish liturgical precedents. It was closely modelled on the Scottish Book of Common Order, a near relative of John Knox's Genevan Service Book. For the deviations from the Scottish norm, Goodwin alone must be held responsible. The Committee prefers a manual to a liturgy, so that by it the ministers may, if need be

have some help and furniture, and yet so as they become not hereby slothful and negligent in stirring up the gifts of Christ in them: but that each one by meditation, by taking heed to himself and the flock of God committed to him, and by wise observing of the ways of Divine Providence, may be careful to furnish his heart and tongue with further or other materials of prayer and exhortation, as shall be needful upon all occasions.[1]

The modifications required in worship are the common-places of Puritan apologetics, and the *Directory* rejected the Apocrypha in the lections, discontinued private baptisms and the practice of having godparents, abolished the sign of the cross in Baptism, and the use of the marriage-ring. The communion-table was moved into the body of the churches, whilst sitting or standing was preferred to kneeling, as the posture for the reception of the sacred elements. Saints' days and creeds were discarded, as were liturgical vestments. No service was appointed for the dead, and no provision was made for the 'churching' of women.

In the *Directory* the Preaching of the Word was given the dignity this ordinance deserves. No longer would the reading of a homily be a surrogate for the glorious gospel of the blessed God: 'Preaching of the Word, being the power of God unto salvation, and one of the greatest and most excellent works belonging to the ministry of the Gospel, should be so performed that the workman need not be ashamed, but may save himself and those that hear him.[2] The *Directory*

[1] Hall, *Reliquiae Liturgicae*, III, p. 18.
[2] *id.*, III, p. 35.

envisages not only a conscientious but also a learned ministry, expert in Hebrew and Greek. The sermons are to be constructed on a threefold mode then current, of Doctrine, Reason, and Use. The discourse therefore begins with clear exposition; then follow the reasons why the doctrine is to be held and a statement of its advantages; and finally an application of the doctrine to the exigencies of everyday life.

On the whole, then, the Westminster Assembly cannot bear comparison with any of the great Church Councils of previous centuries, even though respect may be had for the erudition of its individual members. It was an extremely factious gathering, with 'plots and packing worse than Trent', if Milton is to be believed. It may even be doubted whether its composition of the *Directory*, the *Confession*, and the *Catechisms*, is not more the work of the Scottish Commissioners than of their English brethren. It should be remembered, however, that it was the creation of Parliament and had no legislative authority.

For an outstanding illustration of the greatness of Presbyterianism in England, it is necessary to leave the ecclesiastical diplomats at their noisy logomachy, and to seek out Richard Baxter in the quiet, leafy lanes of Worcestershire, visiting his parishioners on the outskirts of Kidderminster. Averse to the contentiousness of the times, he preferred to describe himself as a 'meer Catholick'.[1] With the Restoration he was, however, to lead the Presbyterians in their attempt to find a formula of comprehension with the Anglican Bishops at the

---

[1] Baxter, like Ussher, believed in a primitive episcopal form of church polity and has, therefore, affinities with Anglicanism and Presbyterianism. His position after the Restoration was that of a Non-conformist.

Savoy Conference. He was both devout and incorruptible, and chose to be ejected under the Clarendon Code, though he might have had a bishopric.

As a pastor, he was unflagging in his zeal, and his labours for his Lord were herculean. In his autobiography, he vividly describes his pastoral work:

I preached before the wars twice each Lord's Day; but after the War but once, and every Thursday, besides occasional Sermons. Every Thursday evening my Neighbours that were most desirous and had opportunity, met at my House, and there one of them repeated the Sermon, and afterwards they proposed what Doubts any of them had about the Sermon, or any other Case of Conscience, and I resolved their Doubts; and last of all, I caused sometimes one, and sometimes another of them to Pray (to exercise them); and sometimes I prayed with them myself; which (besides singing a Psalm) was all they did. And once a Week, also some of the younger sort who were not fit to pray in so great an Assembly met among a few more privately, where they spent three hours in Prayer together. . . . Once in a few Weeks we had a Day of Humiliation on one Occasion or other. . . .[1]

As an organizer, and as a writer, he had outstanding gifts of intellect and spirit. In pursuance of his catholicity, he persuaded the ministers of all the Protestant denominations within the County of Worcestershire to found an ecclesiastical Association in 1653. The first exponent of Ecumenism in England, he claimed that all who accepted the Apostles' Creed as a summary of belief, the Lord's Prayer as a summary of devotion, and the Decalogue as a summary of duty, were truly Christians and members of the Catholic or Universal Church of Christ.

[1] *Reliquiae Baxterianae* (1695), p. 83.

Baxter was equally distinguished as a preacher, combining a profound clarity with psychological insight:

It is no small matter [he wrote] to stand up in the face of a congregation, and deliver a message of salvation or damnation, as from the living God, in the name of our Redeemer. It is no easy matter to speak so plain, that the ignorant may understand us; and so seriously that the deadest hearts may feel us; and so convincingly that contradicting cavillers may be silenced.[1]

His *Reformed Pastor* was the ideal mirror for every minister of the Word of God of his days. His *Christian Directory* seems to have been the first compendium of moral theology produced by any English Protestant, admirable in its spiritual profundity, and in the practical advice in which it abounds. His masterpiece on the devotional life (entitled *The Saint's Everlasting Rest*), bears comparison with that other Puritan classic, *The Pilgrim's Progress*. For him the shining towers of eternity beckoned through the mists of time, as may be discerned in passages of lyrical mysticism like the following:

Thus as Daniel in his captivity did three times a day open his windows to wards Jerusalem, though far out of sight, when he went to God in his devotions; so may the believing soul in this captivity to the flesh look towards Jerusalem which is above . . . And as the pretty lark doth sing most sweetly, and never cease her pleasant ditty while she hovereth aloft, as if she were there gazing into the glory of the sun, but is suddenly silenced when she falleth to the earth: so is the frame of the soul most delectable and divine, whilst she keepeth in the view of

[1] *The Reformed Pastor* (edn. 1860), p. 128.

God by contemplation: but alas, we make there too short
a stay, but down again we fall, and lay by our music.[1]

Presbyterianism, as a religious system in England,
fell for precisely the same reason as the Elizabethan
settlement dissolved, because men and women cannot
be dragooned into a denomination, irrespective of their
religious experiences or predilections. Conformity by
compulsion inevitably produces a defiant Dissent.
Presbyterianism was top-heavy with autocracy, and its
descent was the occasion for the ascent of the Independents. From the beginning they were forced to plead for
religious toleration, in order that they might not be
lopped off in the Procrustean bed of Geneva. They also
knew that the plea for toleration was the cry to which
the Sectaries would rally. Independents were in the
ascendant from 1653 onwards, when Oliver assumed
the office of Lord Protector, mainly because he disliked Presbyterian intolerance as much as he welcomed
the toleration which the Independents made the main
plank in their platform. It was Thomas Goodwin who
showed the absurdity of trying to compel religious
uniformity, claiming that it was as foolish as

to set a company of armed men about an house to keep
darkness out of it in the night season. For as the natural
darknesse cannot be prevented, or dispelled, but by the
presence of light, nor needeth there to be anything,
either for the preventing or dispelling it, but light onely.[2]

Cook, another Independent, put it more bluntly: 'It is
no proper way to confute an heretick, to break his head
with the Bible.' [3] Some of the Independents, when

[1] From the concluding passage of *The Saint's Everlasting
Rest*.
[2] *A Fresh Discovery*, p. 9.
[3] *What the Independents would have* (1647), p. 6.

they came to power, tended to regiment others into
their way of believing, but Goodwin resisted the
temptation to the end, claiming

. . . the professing powers of this world have in all times
itching desires to be officious unto Jesus Christ, and to
obtrude upon Him their own projectors and inventions
to accomodate and help Him through the world with His
worship and Gospel.[1]

The testing-time came with Cromwell's religious
settlement. The Church was to be neither Episcopal,
Presbyterian, nor Independent; but as the apostles of
toleration, the Independents were given favourable
consideration, one of them, John Owen, being
appointed Dean of Christ Church and Vice-Chancellor
of the University of Oxford, whilst another, Thomas
Goodwin, became President of Magdalen. The question was: would the Independents in power prove as
tolerant as when they were in a minority? The Independents exercised their authority by means of two
bodies, which were established with the purpose of
excluding all unworthy ministers, and of admitting to
the ministry suitable candidates. 'The Committee of
Triers' had the responsibility of testing the spiritual
and academic fitness of applicants for the ministry,
and for particular ministerial vacancies. The Commissioners numbered 33 divines and 10 laymen, and
included many Independents, several Presbyterians,
and a few Baptists. Five months later, on 29 August
1654, another Ordinance was promulgated appointing
Lay Commissioners in all the counties of England and
Wales with the power to eject 'scandalous, ignorant and
insufficient ministers and schoolmasters'. There were
15 to 30 laymen on each County Committee, with 8 to

[1] *Basanistai or the Triers*, pp. 17–18.

10 clerical assessors. Patrons retained their right of presentation, whilst Cromwell, in whom were vested the powers of Crown patronage, held half the livings of England in his gift, but the minister being presented could not enter into his living without a certificate of fitness from the Triers. No formal Creed or Confession of Faith was required of the applicants, but the Triers insisted upon the acceptance of the Calvinist theology in broad outline. Even Episcopalians were not excluded, provided they did not use the Book of Common Prayer. Only Roman Catholics were excluded from livings, and these as much from political as from theological reasons. If this did not mean complete toleration, it presented a higher measure of toleration than the State had hitherto allowed in ecclesiastical matters.

Baxter's judgement may stand on the work of the Triers :

The truth is, that though their Authority was null, and though some few over-busy and over-rigid Independents among them were too severe against all that were Arminians, and too particular in enquiring after Evidences of Sanctification in those whom they Examined, and somewhat too lax in their admission of Unlearned and Erroneous Men, that favoured Antinomianism or Anabaptism; yet to give them their due, they did abundance of good to the Church: They saved many a congregation from ignorant, ungodly, drunken Teachers . . . and that sort of Ministers that either preacht against a holy Life, or preacht as Men that never were acquainted with it; all those that used the Ministry but as a Common Trade to live by, and were never likely to convert a soul; all these they usually rejected; and in their stead admitted of any that were able serious Preachers, and lived a godly life, of what tolerable opinion soever they were.[1]

[1] *Reliquiae Baxterianae*, I, 72.

Since they had Baptists on their Committee, it is only to be expected that they should deal leniently with Anabaptists, and, since the three denominations were united in a Calvinistic theology, that this should be their doctrinal test. At the same time, a number of pronounced Episcopalians were allowed to retain their livings, even though they were known to be unfavourable to the Government.

Walker's estimate in his *Sufferings of the Clergy* [1] that 6,000 or 7,000 episcopalian priests were ejected by the Triers, though it has been doubted, appears substantially accurate as a result of the researches of A. G. Matthews.[2] What is more important to ascertain is whether in fact they were ejected for good and sufficient reasons. Once again Baxter may be cited as witness:

> I must needs say, that in all the Counteys where I was acquainted . . ., six to one at least (if not many more) that were Sequestered by the Committee, were by the Oaths of Witnesses proved insufficient, or scandalous, or both; especially guilty of Drunkenness or Swearing: and those that being able, godly Preachers, were cast out for the War alone, as for their Opinions' sake, were comparatively very few.[3]

Certainly the Puritans would have been fortunate to receive as just a treatment, at the hands of the Episcopalians, when the monarchy was restored.

Independents increased in numbers and in influence in these days. Whilst Owen and Goodwin held high positions, as Heads of Houses in Oxford, they and John Howe [4] also were Cromwell's chaplains; meanwhile Caryll and Nye occupied London rectories.

---

[1] I, pp. 199–200.   [2] *Walker Revised* (1948), p. xiii.
[3] *Reliquiae Baxterianae*, I, p. 74.
[4] Howe was a Presbyterian with Independent sympathies.

Numerically, Independency (or Congregationalism) was not strong, for when the Savoy Conference was held in 1658 only 120 Churches sent delegates. Allowing for the fact that 360 ministers ejected during the imposition of the Clarendon Code claimed to be Independent or Congregational, it is probable that the combined membership of all the churches of this persuasion did not exceed 50,000 souls. Their importance is to be found in three elements: first, their ministers were both fearless and erudite; they were the apostles of toleration in a country torn by Civil War; thirdly, they attracted to their camp two of the most important laymen of the age, Milton and Cromwell. Apart from their claim for the freedom of conscience and the entire separation of the spheres of Church and State, they had little of distinction to contribute. The Savoy Declaration of 1658 is, it must be confessed, largely a duplicate of the Westminster Confession, with the exception of its noble preamble, distinguishing between a Creed as a prescribed form, and a Declaration as a statement of terms of Communion.

The true greatness of Independency is seen, it has been suggested, in the distinction of two of its sons, renowned in the history of England. John Milton believed that truth was indomitable, and that the attempt to coerce truth was an admission of dubiety. His advocacy of an unlicensed right to publish books is one of the noblest pleas of English history: 'And though all the winds of doctrine were let loose to play upon the earth, so truth be in the field, we do injuriously by licensing and prohibiting to misdoubt her strength. Let truth and falsehood grapple; who ever knew truth put to the worse in a free and open encounter?' [1] True

[1] *Areopagitica* (*Milton's Prose Works*, Bohn edn., II, p. 96).

religion is for him the service of God, not in the
externals of ceremonial or vestments. His creed is best
given in his own poetry:

> Henceforth I learn that to obey is best,
> And love with fear the only God, to walk
> As in his presence, ever to observe
> His providence, and on him sole depend,
> Merciful over all his works, with good
> Still overcoming evil, and by small
> Accomplishing great things, by things deemed weak
> Subverting worldly strong, and worldly wise
> By simply meek; that suffering for truth's sake
> Is fortitude to highest victory,
> And, to the faithful, death the gate of life;
> Taught this by his example whom I now
> Acknowledge my Redeemer ever blest.

This dedicated spirit vowed at the age of twenty-three:

> All is, if I have grace to use it so,
> As ever in my great Task-Master's eye.

He united the contemplative and the active life as epic
poet and as Latin—that is, Foreign—Secretary to the
Commonwealth. Milton's poetry and his life breathe
the virility, integrity, and independence of Puritanism.

Oliver Cromwell, the other distinguished Independent, is a complex figure. The outstanding apostle of
toleration and liberty, he yet snatched more power than
any other commoner in the history of England. There
can be no doubt that he was, at heart, more tolerant
than most of his times. He hoped for a union of all
godly people, 'Scotts, English, Jewes, Gentiles, Presb^{ns},
Independents, Anabaptists & all'.[1] In pursuance of
this policy, he formulated a church settlement in which

---

[1] *Clarke Papers*, ii, pp. 51–2.

there should be no established church in England, presenting the livings in his power to the men thought to be the most conscientious and able ministers, irrespective of denominations. He also, in the same spirit, readmitted the Jews into England in 1657. The army's plea for toleration addressed to the autocratic Presbyterians, some years earlier, shows the influence of their Commander-in-Chief:

Are we to be dealt with as enemies because we come not to your way? Is all religion wrapt up in that or any form? Does that name or thing give the difference between those that are members of Christ and those that are not? We think not so. We say faith, working by love, is the true character of the Christian, and God is our witness, in whomsoever we see any of Christ to be, these we reckon our duty to love, waiting for a more plentiful effusion of the spirit of God to make all Christians to be of one heart.[1]

In his theory of toleration, there is evidence of many diverse sources which contributed to his thinking. The main source is his religious faith, holding that all men are competent to discover divine truth, and must be allowed to proceed in the way that God has ordained for them. The clergy had distorted and complicated an essentially simple faith, and turned a means of communion with God into a tyrannical prescription. There was blended in the crucible of his thought on toleration

the sectarian devotion to religious liberty on the grounds of moral right, the lay distrust of clerical bigotry, the Latitudinarian conviction that all Christians who profess

[1] *Declaration of the Army of England* (1650) in S.P. Dom. Commonwealth and Protectorate, IX, p. 114.

the fundamentals of faith are in a substantial unity, and
the Erastian determination to preserve to mankind the
benefits of intellectual and spiritual freedom through the
restraint of clerical arrogance.[1]

Although his work appeared to be overwhelmed at the
Restoration, with the return of the monarchy and the
Anglican Establishment, the monarchy was henceforth
to be tamed by Parliament, and the Dissenters, given
encouragement during the days of Cromwell's power,
were to play an increasingly important part in the
political and religious life of England.

Cromwell shared in a peculiar measure the Puritan
doctrines of Election and Providence. He was nerved
to undertake tasks before which other men would have
quailed, because he had a conviction of being an instrument of righteousness in the hand of God, a chosen
spirit. His combination of piety and prudence is seen
at the battle of Dunbar, when, having beaten the enemy
with a loss of under twenty of his own men, compared
with the three thousand of the enemy slain and ten
thousand captives, he made a brief halt during the
prolonged chase and called for the singing of the
briefest psalm of thanksgiving. As a true Puritan he
was often found 'waiting upon God', and searching for
His hand in the events of the day. On one famous
occasion, when he was convinced of God's displeasure
with his army for their temporizing with the King, he
convened the entire army to a prayer-meeting, and they
spent the whole day in devotions and a cross-examina-
tion of their consciences, whilst on the following day
Cromwell exhorted them to make: 'a thorough consideration of our actions as an Army, and of our ways

[1] Jordan, *The Development of Religious Toleration in England*,
III, pp. 145–6.

particularly as private Christians'.[1] Cromwell served his people best, he realized, as the servant of the King of kings.

As we have seen in earlier chapters, the Puritan was distinguished by his adherence to the pure Word of God, his Scripturism. But there were two other ways in which he might also learn the will of God. He believed in religious experience, practical mysticism, in which God might choose to reveal himself to the soul, and he regarded events as being a testimony to God. The life of Dissent during this period is an antinomy of individualism and of communal expectations. The explanation of these divergent emphases, individual and corporate, is found in the doctrine of Election. The Puritan had a sense of special knowledge of and co-operation with the purposes of God, but he was a member of the Elect Community, the Church of the Saints of God. This sense of election nerved him in the severest ordeals, and was the mainspring of his zeal for reform. His life was active rather than contemplative, though he was capable of the most profound scrutiny of his motives. Nevertheless, most Puritans would have agreed with Baxter that 'It is by action that God is most served and honoured.'[2] The main difficulty of the Puritan was to balance the claims of reform and of liberty. If the Presbyterians erred on the side of reform, the Independents and the sectaries overstressed liberty to the point of anarchy. It is certain, however, that it is in this period that the cry of liberty of conscience was first raised, and that a segregation of Church and State was proposed by Independents and Baptists to preserve

[1] See the present writer's *The Worship of the English Puritans*, pp. 283-4. [2] *Christian Directory*, I, p. 336.

G

the liberty of the individual conscience. Perhaps the most distinctive contribution of Puritanism to English life is found in the literal application of the doctrine of the priesthood of all believers. This was first enunciated by Luther, but both Lutherans and Calvinists, not to mention the Anglicans, had given the State and the magistrate powers over the Church. It was the glory of the Independent churches to give to all their members, regardless of personal rank or sex, equal rights in the government of their congregations.[1] Egalitarianism was only the secularization of the doctrine of the priesthood of all believers. In one other respect, also, the Independent churches (and the Baptists followed their ecclesiastical order), were to make a significant contribution to political life. Each Independent church was founded upon a covenant, in which the members promised to assist one another in walking in God's ways. These ecclesiastical covenants helped, by analogy, to establish in the civil sphere the doctrine of the social contract and of government by consent. Moreover, the local congregation was the school of democracy, for, according to Lord Lindsay:

There the humblest member might lead and join in the debate, might witness the discovery of the natural leader, and participate in that curious process by which there emerges from the clash of many minds a vision clearer and a determination wiser than any single man could achieve. To the congregation we may look for the source and model of that democratic organization and practice of which the recorded proceedings of the General Council of the Army are the most striking examples.[2]

[1] It should be pointed out, however, that the minister and ruling elders in Congregational churches had a real, if representative and delegated, authority over the church members.
[2] *The Essentials of Democracy*, pp. 11 ff.

CHAPTER V

UNDER THE CROSS OF PERSECUTION

THE Independents, as the churchmen most highly favoured by the late Protector, had little to hope for in the arrival of Charles II, except perhaps toleration. The Baptists were in similar case. The Quakers could not be described as regicides, since they became an active organization only in the closing years of the Protectorate, and won only a grudging toleration from Cromwell. By the country at large, however, they were regarded as eccentrics who refused to take oaths or to doff their caps to magistrates, and were potentially the overthrowers of all authority in Church and State. Of the non-Anglican Churches the Presbyterians had the most reason to regard the future with optimism. They were in ecclesiastical possession at the time of the King's return; they were Erastians; General Monk, who engineered the Restoration, proclaimed his sympathy with them rather than with the Independents in reconstituting the Long Parliament. The more realistic amongst them recognized that a State Presbyterianism would not be the order of the new day, but they hoped for comprehension within a national Church which would combine a modified episcopacy with a modified presbyteral system. In the strength of this hope, and their strategic position, they welcomed the Restoration.

At first Charles received them with respect and gave them recognition by offering to appoint several of their number court chaplains, though only four of them —namely, Reynolds, Calamy, Spurstow, and Baxter —seem to have officiated. A group of moderate

Presbyterians met, with royal sanction, in Sion College, where, after a debate of three weeks, they prepared an address to the King, proposing that Archbishop Ussher's *Reduction of Episcopacy unto the form of Synodical Government, received in the Ancient Church,* should form the basis of agreement between Presbyterians and Anglicans.

The King seemed to accede to the Presbyterian demands by authorizing the convocation of the Savoy Conference, in which twelve bishops and twelve Presbyterian ministers were to consider the comprehension of the Presbyterians in the Establishment. The Conference commenced on 15 April 1661 and was expected to continue for four months. Sheldon, the chairman, manœuvred the Presbyterians into the position of petitioners, giving the impression that it was a condescension to treat with them. The sole fruit of this abortive meeting was the production of the 'Reformed Liturgy' by Richard Baxter, as a reply to the scathing episcopal request that if the Presbyterians found the Prayer Book so exceptionable, they should provide their own. Apart from its innate merits, this liturgy proved that the Presbyterians had no objection to set prayers as such, but could not agree that the Book of Common Prayer was in all things conformable to the Word of God. In short, the Presbyterians were making a great concession in discussing a modified episcopal government in the national Church, whilst the bishops would make none.

Meanwhile, Parliamentary legislation against the Dissenters was being promulgated, which underlined the futility of further conference with the Anglicans, and the inconsistency of the King. The first lash of the five-stringed whip (as the Clarendon Code was known) was the Corporation Act of 1661, which prohibited any

Nonconformist henceforth from holding office in any
city or municipal corporation, a ban that fell heavily on
the Presbyterians in particular, because many of them
held office in the City of London, and in other corporations. This, however, was only the beginning of the
persecution. The most serious attack was on the ranks
of the dissident ministers themselves, which followed in
1662, in the humiliating Act of Uniformity.

The two main provisions of this Act were to require
all ministers to be re-ordained, if they had not pre-
viously been episcopally ordained, and to declare their
'unfeigned assent and consent' to the Book of Common
Prayer, as in all things agreeable to the Word of God.
Subsidiary requirements were that they should take an
oath of canonical obedience to their ordinary, and to
abjure the Solemn League and Covenant. This was
passed on 19 May and was to take effect on 24 August
1662. That being St. Bartholomew's Day, the event
was inevitably linked with the wholesale massacre of the
Huguenots, and excellent use of this coincidence was
made by Nonconformist propagandists. It was an Act
that made it impossible for ministers of conscience to
conform. It aimed at compelling religious uniformity;
it succeeded in consolidating religious Nonconformity
as a force in the national life of England.

There were manifold reasons why Presbyterians,
Independents, and Baptists found themselves unable to
conform. Re-ordination was offensive because it im-
plied a renunciation of the validity of their existing
Orders, and a disowning of the fruits of their ministries.
Since the days of the Hampton Court Conference, all
Dissenters had been united in the conviction that the
Prayer Book did not conform to the Word of God in
several important particulars. In fact, the different

denominations existed to provide a worship and polity which seemed to them warranted by the Holy Scriptures. In the third place, the request for their abjuration of the Solemn League and Covenant constituted a demand for pledge-breaking, whereas a more delicate reading of the situation would have asked only for a declaration of loyalty to the King. The greatest difficulty was found in the request that they concur in the purity of the Prayer Book. This was, in effect, a demand that they entirely recant their Puritanism. They could not do this since the Book of Common Prayer obliged them to use the sign of the cross in Baptism, to reject all who would not kneel for the reception of the Lord's Supper, to pronounce (with some few exceptions) that all that were buried were saved, to read lessons from the Apocrypha and to recite the damnatory clauses in the Athanasian Creed, and finally to prescribe the use of godparents to the exclusion of parents in Baptism.

It is worth comparing the reasons for nonconformity adduced by the Presbyterian divine, John Howe, with those of the Independent minister, John Owen. Howe's unwillingness to conform is based upon three grounds: he could not submit to re-ordination nor to the absolute enforcement of ceremonies not warranted by the Word of God, and he found the Anglican Church unable or unwilling to exercise a strong scriptural discipline for the maintenance of the purity of its church members.[1] Owen confines himself, in the main, to an attack on the iniquity of the imposition of a Liturgy. The imposition of the Liturgy has, so he claims, three disastrous results: it leads to the atrophy of spiritual gifts and to 'men napkining their talents'; the uniformity of a

[1] *Works* (ed. Hewlett), I, p. xviii.

liturgy makes impossible the application of grace to the varying needs of different congregations; it abridges the liberty of the disciples of Christ in unnecessary matters.[1] Moreover, in the past such impositions had 'brought fire and faggot in their train'.

The Nonconformist ministers, now to be ejected in their hundreds, took their stand upon the supremacy of the revelation of God over the prudential dictates of men, and upon the liberty of Christians infringed by the imposition of indifferent ceremonies. To have conformed would have been to deny their heritage and to muffle their consciences taken captive by the Word of God. The Great Ejection of 1662 was, given the intransigent terms of the Act of Uniformity, inevitable. For most Nonconformist ministers it was a journey into impenetrable darkness. They could hardly know that, as they left their beloved flocks and renounced their means of subsistence, their churches would conform to the inevitable Christian pattern of resurrection through death, and that the effect of the Act of Uniformity would be to establish and consolidate Nonconformity. It was sufficient for them to walk by faith, and not by sight.

The immediate result of the imposition of the Act of Uniformity was the ejection of a fifth of the divines of England from their pastoral charges or academic posts.[2] Most of them were not only more conscientious but more learned than their Anglican counterparts. Of the 1,603 ejected about whom there is available detailed information, A. G. Matthews has established that 1,285 had received university education. Of this number 733 had been educated at Cambridge, 513 at Oxford, 20 at

[1] *Works* (ed. Goold), xv, pp. 52 ff.
[2] A. G. Matthews, *Calamy Revised*.

the Scottish universities, 12 at Harvard, and 2 at Trinity
College, Dublin. Eleven Heads of Colleges and Halls,
39 resident Fellows, 3 non-resident Fellows, and 3
College chaplains were removed from Oxford in 1660,
whilst 3 Heads of Colleges and 4 Fellows were ejected
from the same university in 1662. In Cambridge 5
Heads of Colleges, 18 Fellows, and 2 College chaplains
were removed in 1660, and 1 Head and 14 Fellows two
years later. The Headmaster and 5 Fellows of Eton
suffered the same fate in 1660. In all, 149 divines holding academic positions were ejected at, or soon after,
the Restoration. Whilst many of these were to place
their learning and experience at the disposal of the
Dissenting Academies and to write a new chapter in
the history of modern education in England, their loss
was a grievous wound to the Establishment and helped
to account for the torpor of the ancient universities at
the end of the century, and during the later time of
Gibbon's tutelage. It is no exaggeration, therefore, to
describe the Great Ejection as 'that stroke of palsy for
the Anglican Church and of painful birth for genuine
Free Churchmanship'.[1]

The plight of Nonconformist divines, without private
means, was pathetic. The story may be read in
Calamy's *History of the Ejected Ministers* of their pitiful
shifts in penury, dependent upon a hand-to-mouth
existence and compelled to become mendicants. Many
were forced to take up other dissimilar means of earn-
ing a livelihood. John Goodwin, former Independent
divine and strongest protagonist of toleration, became
the proprietor of an eating-house. Others were less
adaptable and therefore harder hit. Baxter once met
the Bishop of Chichester, Dr. Gunning, when walking

[1] *Essays Congregational and Catholic*, ed. A. Peel (1931).

in the fields outside London. The bishop asserted that the Nonconformists 'were fed as full and lived as much to the pleasure of the flesh in plenty as the Conformists did', to which the Presbyterian divine retorted that 'he was a stranger to the men he talked of'. He then adds:

I had but a few days before had letters of a worthy minister who, with his wife and six children, had many years had seldom other food than brown rye-bread and water, and was then turned out of his house, and had none to go to. And of another that was fain to spin for his living. And abundance I know that have families, and nothing or next to nothing of their own, and live in exceeding want upon the poor drops of charity which they stoop to receive from a few mean people.[1]

To their sufferings the Nonconformist divines were to add a further proof of their sincerity and courage. This opportunity came with the Plague of 1665, and is best described in Baxter's own words:

And when the plague grew hot most of the conformable ministers fled, and left their flocks in the time of their extremity, whereupon divers Nonconformists, pitying the dying and distressed people that had none to call the impenitent to repentance, nor to help men to prepare for another world, nor to comfort them in their terrors, when about ten thousand died in a week, resolved that no obedience to the laws of any mortal men whosoever could justify them for neglecting of men's souls and bodies in such extremities, no more than they can justify parents for famishing their children to death. And that when Christ shall say, 'Inasmuch as ye did it not to one of these, ye did it not to me', it will be a poor excuse to say, 'Lord, I was forbidden by the law'.[2]

[1] *The Autobiography of Richard Baxter*, p. 223.
[2] *op. cit.*, p. 196.

The Act of Uniformity was followed by other legislation designed to break the spirit of the Nonconformists. The Conventicle Act of 1664 rendered illegal
the gathering of five or more persons over the age of
sixteen under the colour of religion. A fine of £5 was
imposed for the first breach of the law, and for the
third offence the penalty was transportation to a
colonial plantation other than Virginia or New England.
In 1665 there followed the Act for restraining Nonconformists from inhabiting Corporations, commonly
called the Five Mile Act. It forbade all preachers and
teachers who refused the oaths to come within five
miles of any corporate town. Such persons, and any
who refused to attend worship at a parish church, were
prohibited from teaching, under a penalty of £40,
whether as schoolmasters or private tutors.

Despite the general stringency of the law, here and
there it was evaded by ingenious stratagems. The combined congregation of Baptists and Presbyterians meeting at Broadmead, Bristol, hit on the device of singing
psalms immediately they were warned of the approach
of informers. Their plans were carefully laid:

And when we had notice that the informers or officers
were coming, we caused the minister or brother that
preached, to forbear and sit down. Then we drew back
the curtain, laying the whole room open, that they might
see us all. And so all the people begin to sing a psalm,
that, at the beginning of the meeting we did always name
the psalm we would sing, if the informers or the Mayor
or his officers come in. Thus still when they came in we
were singing, that they could not find anyone preaching,
but all singing. And, at our meeting, we ordered it so,
that none read the psalm after the first line, but everyone
brought their bible, and so read for themselves; that they
might not lay hold of any one for preaching, or as much

as reading the psalm, and so to imprison any more for that, as they had our ministers.[1]

Another congregation, meeting in St. Thomas's, Southwark, almost whispered the psalms to avoid attracting attention. A report of this conventicle states:

> 1692. April 1st. We met at Mr. Russell's in Ironmonger Lane, where Mr. Lambert of Deadman's Place, Southwark, administered to us the ordinance of the Lord's Supper, and we sang a psalm in a low voice.[2]

Many were the devices employed to escape the long arm of the law. Richard Chantrey, ejected from the Shropshire chapel of Welford, dressed as an agricultural labourer, with a fork over his shoulder and a Bible in his pocket, and thus made his way to the conventicles at which he preached. Dissenters in the South Midlands used to meet near Olney at a place known as Three Counties Point, where Northamptonshire, Buckinghamshire, and Bedfordshire adjoined. If attacked from either side it was an easy matter to escape over the border into another county.[3]

Thomas Jollie, of the Northern counties, stood outside a door whose top half was set on hinges, so that the room could be immediately hidden from any intruder ascending the stairs, and preached to an audience within the room itself.[4] A more common device was to hide the door of a room used for worship by moving a great cupboard against the entrance. Sometimes a table was spread with food, so that, in an emergency, a religious gathering might be made to look like a festive company.[4] In those days of persecution, worship was held

---

[1] *Broadmead Records* (ed. Underhill), p. 226.
[2] Curwen, *Studies in Music & Worship*, p. 84.
[3] Whiting, *Studies in English Puritanism*, p. 60.
[4] Clark, *History of English Nonconformity*, II, pp. 67–9.

in the dead of night, in the open air, in woods or orchards, in shops or barns, in underground recesses or vaults. It was a return to the Church of the catacombs. The toponymy of England gives in such place-names as Gospel Beech, or Gospel Oak, testimony to the resourcefulness of proscribed conventiclers in the seventeenth century. The Quakers, however, who refused to take cover, bore the full brunt of the persecution.

The last step in the logic of persecution was to prohibit Dissenters from occupying any post whether civil, naval, or military, under the aegis of the government. Thus the Test Act of 1673 may be regarded as the extension of the provisions of the Corporation Act of 1661. Short of wholesale execution or exile, the legislature had tried every means to suppress Nonconformity. The short lulls in the persecution only served to show that Dissent had not gone to its grave, it had merely gone to earth. As soon as it was given toleration, hundreds of Nonconformist Churches were founded, and hundreds of meeting-houses were erected. The single effect of toleration was to make a *de facto* Dissent *de jure*.

Before the passing of the Act of Uniformity there were doubtless many formal Dissenters, but afterwards none, for the flail of persecution separated the wheat from the chaff. Now the Nonconformists learned the meaning of entering into the sufferings of Christ. They emerged in 1689 as a purified and convinced remnant. If the Churches in times of State promotion and favour develop in extent and widen their influence, in times of State persecution they develop in depth and intensity. Baxter, in a prolonged self-analysis during the time of persecution, claims: 'The tenor of the Gospel predictions, precepts, promises and threatenings are fitted to a people in a suffering state. And the graces of God in a believer are mostly suited to a state of suffering. Christians must imitate Christ, and suffer with Him before they reign with Him; and His kingdom was not of this world.' [1] John Howe writes in the same strain: 'Every sincere Christian is in affection and preparation of his mind a martyr. He that loves not Christ better than his own life, cannot be His disciple.' [2] A proof that persecution deepened personal religion during the Restoration can be found in the quality of the devotional treatises of the period. Baxter's *Now or Never*, Alleine's *Call to the Unconverted*, John Howe's *The Living Temple*, John Owen's *A Discourse of the Work of the Holy Spirit in Prayer*, and Bunyan's *Grace Abounding to the Chief of Sinners* are the by-products of persecution. At this time also the greatest of Puritan poets, John Milton, overcame his blindness and disappointment at the turn of events in the composition of *Paradise Lost* and *Samson Agonistes*. These are plummets sounding the uttermost depths of Puritan religious experience.

Persecution had the further effect of driving Independents and Presbyterians into one another's arms as companions in suffering. Indeed, their ties with the Baptists were closer during this period. It cannot be doubted that if the Presbyterian proposals had been accepted by the Savoy Conference, and if they had been included within the national Church, the other Nonconformist denominations, numerically inferior, would have waited perhaps for a century or more before winning the limited rights of toleration. In unity, however, they were a significant minority. The proof of the growing unity between the Dissenting denominations is

[1] *The Autobiography of Richard Baxter*, p. 122.
[2] Cited R. F. Horton, *John Howe* (1894).

seen in the famous *Heads of Agreement*, proposals for
the effective practical co-operation of Presbyterians and
Independents. These proposals were agreed to by over
100 ministers of the two denominations in the City of
London, and the scheme spread immediately to the
provinces. Party-cries were dropped, the beating of the
denominational drum was silenced, and the co-operating ministers worked together from 1690 to 1694 as the
'United Brethren'. It may be represented as a tamed
Presbyterianism, because the Churches were 'Gathered
Churches', i.e. a combination of contiguous and convinced Christian families gathered by Christ out of the
world, but the Independents recognized the advisory
authority of neighbouring Churches in the selection of
their ministers. Concessions, as is inevitable in any
ecumenical advance, were made on both sides. The
'Happy Union' disintegrated after only four years as
the result of a doctrinal controversy, in which certain
Independents out-Calvinized the Presbyterians. After
bitter mutual recrimination, the two denominations
went their separate ways in London, but the association
continued to flourish in the provinces. Closer co-operation between Baptists, Independents, and Presbyterians
was to bear fruit in the formation in 1732 of the
body known as 'The Dissenting Deputies', whose task
it was to defend Nonconformist civil rights, and
which was given the privilege of direct access to the
sovereign.

Persecution under the Stuarts was succeeded by
toleration under William III. Consequently the Dissenters associated tyranny with the Tories, and liberty
with the Whigs. For this reason Nonconformity threw
in its lot with the Whigs of the eighteenth century and
the Liberals of the nineteenth. The beginning of the

famous 'Nonconformist conscience' derives, therefore, from the Act of Toleration in 1689. Charles I had declared that 'Presbyterianism was no religion for gentlemen', and Presbyterians hailed the arrival of William, as a member of the Reformed Church of Holland. The two other Free Churches had already proved, by their type of church government, which gave complete expression to the Reformation doctrine of the priesthood of all believers, that they were the friends of democracy. In the last resort, the fact that radical movements in English politics were never anti-clerical, as on the Continent, may be traced to the Non-conformist love of liberty born in the days of the Clarendon Code. In addition, the end of the seven-teenth century sees the beginning of the distinction between a 'church' and a 'chapel' ethos and culture. According to Dr. G. N. Clark: 'It became one of the dividing lines in party politics, in the press, and in everything else, even in economic life.' [1] The sobriety, frugality, and industry fostered in Puritanism were conducive to business success, and it is no accident that from this time onward we read of Quakers, Baptists, and other sectaries, as successful manufacturers, bankers, and business-men. This distinctive culture and outlook, manifested in a deepening sense of tolera-tion, with a deep ethical seriousness and scepticism of tradition and authority, was in part bred by the modern education of the Dissenting Academies, contrasted with the traditional disciplines of the ancient universities, although something of the same spirit was evident in the founding of the Royal Society soon after the Restoration. Another historian, Mr. David Ogg, says: 'As nowhere else men acquired the habit of thinking for

[1] *The Later Stuarts*, p. 23.

themselves.' Insistence upon uniformity served only to
strengthen disagreement, and to Clarendon may be
attributed 'some responsibility for the entrenchment in
our national life of the one native institution which no
foreigner can hope to copy—the nonconformist conscience.' [1] To sum up, the Clarendon Code had united
Nonconformity, helped to deepen personal religion by
the stimulus of persecution, and assisted the growth of
toleration, though its objects had been the exact
opposite. Dr. Dale's words are not too strong: 'It was
the salvation of Evangelicalism when the Evangelicals
were rejected.' [2]

Besides the ordinary clergy, there were many Heads
of Colleges and Fellows whom the Restoration and the
Act of Uniformity dispossessed of their places. These
academics, excluded from the ancient universities, used
to receive in their homes the sons of the dissenting
nobility and gentry who wished to provide them with a
liberal education and their pastors with a competence.
The same tutors also gave theological training to those
who, even in the days of persecution, sought to become
Nonconformist ministers. From such lowly beginnings
did the Dissenting Academies rise. In contrast to the
tradition of the ancient Universities, a clear line of
influence can be traced from Comenius, the apostle of
realism and observation, to Hartlib the friend of Milton,
and the Dissenting Academies, which first taught a
broad and progressive curriculum. In one sense the
Dissenting Academies were only putting into practice
what Milton had advocated in his *Tractate on Education* in 1639. They were the grammar schools and

[1] *England in the Reign of Charles II*, 1, p. 218.
[2] *The History of English Congregationalism*, p. 421.

universities which he had envisaged as replacing the ancient universities.

During the period from 1663 to 1690, when the academies were necessarily private and usually staffed by one tutor, in the person of an ejected minister, at least twenty-three are known to have existed. The two most famous were located at Newington on the northern outskirts of the City of London. One of them was known as Morton's Academy, Stoke Newington, the principal being Charles Morton, a distinguished mathematician and Fellow of Wadham College, Oxford, who had learned from the lips of Sir Christopher Wren. He left England in 1685 and, later, became Vice-president of Harvard College. Two of his best known students were Daniel Defoe, political pamphleteer and author of *Robinson Crusoe*, and Samuel, the father of John and Charles Wesley. Samuel Wesley, who later became a trenchant critic of the academies when he joined the Establishment, mentions that several sons of baronets and knights were pupils, and supplies an interesting description of the scientific apparatus of the institution: 'This academy was indeed the most considerable, having annext a fine Garden, Bowling Green, Fish Pond, and within a Laboratory, and some not inconsiderable rarities, with air-pump, thermometer, and all sorts of mathematical instruments.' [1] Such apparatus is a clear indication that mathematics, physics, botany, and zoology were taught there. Of equal importance is the information that democratic responsibility was delegated to the students; each man was allowed to propose disciplinary regulations and to

[1] cf. Irene Parker, *Dissenting Academies in England*, p. 59, to whom the author is greatly indebted for information on this topic.

H

vote his approval or disapproval of penalties imposed for disobedience. The other distinguished alumnus of this academy, Defoe, says that he learned five languages, and studied there political science, mathematics, natural philosophy, logic, geography, and history, and claims that this education was superior to that of the universities, except for the lack of stimulating conversation.

The other institution referred to, housed in Newington Green, was Gale's Academy. Its principal, Theophilus Gale, had been a Fellow of Magdalen College, Oxford. Wood, the biographer of Oxford worthies, describes him as 'an exact philologist and philosopher'. His successor, Thomas Rowe, numbered amongst his pupils Isaac Watts, Daniel Neal (historian of the Puritans), and Josiah Hort who became the Archbishop of Tuam.

The popularity and even respectability of the academies is shown by the fact that John Woodhouse, tutor of the Sheriffhales Academy, had as pupils Robert Harley (later Earl of Oxford) and Henry St. John (later Earl of Bolingbroke). They so far forgot their indebtedness as to be guilty of the rudest ingratitude in introducing the Schism Bill of 1714, aimed at the entire abolition of Dissenting Academies, which only the death of the Queen obstructed.

Under the encouragement of the Hanoverian dynasty, the Academies went from strength to strength. They now became public and more influential institutions, increasing their staff to cope with the greater influx of students. The Tewkesbury Academy, which flourished from 1680 to 1719 under the tuition of Simon Jones, included amongst its students Secker, the future Primate of England, and Butler, future Bishop of Durham and author of *The Analogy of Religion*. The most renowned of the later academies, was, of course, that established at Northampton under the guidance of Dr. Philip Doddridge, which gave individual tuition to backward students and prepared the sons of the gentry and the middle-classes for professional and commercial careers. The Act of Uniformity was not least a gain to modern education in England.

The real strength of Nonconformity during this period is laid bare in the virility and spirituality of the men it bred, leaders of the Free Churches under duress: George Fox, founder and leader of the Quakers; Bunyan, immortal allegorist and moving preacher, amongst the Baptists; Peter Sterry, scholar and mystic of the Independent persuasion; and John Howe, theologian and champion of the Presbyterians. Many other names might be added to the constellation of Nonconformist worthies of the age, such as William Penn, the Admiral's son who became a Quaker and founded in Pennsylvania in the New World the first completely tolerant state, John Owen, the veteran Independent theologian and controversialist, and Philip Henry, distinguished father of a distinguished son, of the Presbyterians, but these representative men must suffice.

George Fox (1624-91) was the son of a Leicestershire weaver and Puritan. He lived from 1643 to 1647 under a deep spiritual depression, seeking enlightenment from the different churches and sects of the Commonwealth. He found the Puritans hypocritical and censorious; the clergy frivolous, mercenary, and vindictive; the Calvinists pessimistic; the opposing parties of the Civil War fratricidal; and he experienced a deep sense of the sufferings of humanity. In his own words he tells of how this seeker became a finder:

108 THE ENGLISH FREE CHURCHES

When all my hopes in them and all men were gone, so that I had nothing outwardly to help me, nor could I tell what to do, then I heard a voice which said, 'There is one, even Christ Jesus, that can speak to thy condition'; and when I heard it, my heart did leap for joy. Then the Lord let me see why there was none upon the earth that could speak to my condition, namely, that I might give Him all the glory.[1]

Fox made it his life-work to reform a half-pagan society by the light and power of the indwelling spirit of Christ. He was acutely sensitive to the injustices and needs of his fellow men, and exhibited a rare courage in acting promptly in conformity with his convictions. He spent eight years incarcerated in prisons as widespread as Nottingham, Derby, Lancaster, Scarborough, Worcester, and Launceston. As a pioneer of social reform, he interested himself deeply in the cause of the poor and aged, prisoners, the American Indians, and the insane. He was outspoken in his opposition to drunkenness, slavery, and capital punishment. His influence in social ethics was considerable, for he believed in the one-price system for trade, and in just wages for working people. He was opposed to oaths and to every kind of war, declaring that he 'lived in the virtue of that life and power that took away the occasion of all wars'.[2] He believed in the religious equality of all men, expressing this in a democratic form of organization in which women, equally with men, were encouraged to give their testimony. In the same spirit he insisted upon simple dress and the use of singular pronouns in addressing all classes of people, and a similar motive

[1] Cited Elbert Russell, *The History of Quakerism,* p. 25.
[2] George Fox, *Journal,* ed. Penney (1924), p. 36.

underlay his refusal to doff the hat to all whom the
world would have regarded as his social and political
superiors. Furthermore, he anticipated John Wesley in
regarding the world as his parish, by travelling over
most of England, Scotland, Ireland, New England, the
West Indies, and Holland. He supplied the normative
Quaker type of religious experience and its fundamental
ideas, became its leading preacher, set up its first
organizations, wrote a distinguished part of its literature, and bore the brunt of the sufferings of the Society
of Friends.

Contrary to common belief the early Quakers were
orthodox Trinitarians in doctrine, as was manifested in
their statement of faith made in 1671 to the Governor
and Council of Barbados.[1] The distinction of Fox and
his followers was that they rediscovered the practical
implications of the Christian doctrine of the Holy
Spirit. This experimental knowledge of the Holy Spirit
they described as 'the Inner Light'. Fox describes
rather than defines the meaning of this term in the
following passage: 'Now the Lord God opened to me
by His invisible power, that every man was enlightened
by the divine light of Christ and I saw it shine through
all; and they that believed in it came out of condemnation to the light of life . . . I was sent to turn people
from darkness to light.'[1] This belief stressed the im-
manence of God as knowable by and within men. It
is only a short step from the inner light to the outer
darkness, but the Quakers were prevented from taking
it by their Calvinistic background, with its emphasis on
the transcendent sovereignty of God. The belief in the
inner light presupposed the capacity of all men to
recognize and respond to God's revelation of love, and

[1] Fox, *op. cit.*, pp. 289-90.

was a direct denial that this ability was limited, as Calvinism taught, to the elect, who alone were assisted by prevenient grace. The inner light is also the description of man's interior and experimental knowledge of God. The doctrine and experience had as its consequences the conviction that communion with God cannot be restricted to time or place, to a priestly caste or sacraments, or to a Bible, indispensable guide as that is. Believing that all men were capable of receiving revelation provided the basis of a universal philanthropy and a complete democracy. The Quakers were religious levellers, and their mysticism was social in character and influence.

Their numbers have been small, not because they were exclusive, but because their standards of conduct and their level of spiritual attainment have been so high. It seems as if the Beatitude 'Blessed are the peacemakers' was reserved especially for their advent, so notable has been their witness to peace through the centuries, maintained in the twentieth century through the Friends' Ambulance Unit and the Fellowship of Reconciliation.[1] Their contribution to the easing of the tension between employer and employee has not been less distinguished in modern days. Frys, Rowntrees, and Cadburys are Quakers who may be said to have sweetened both diet and business relationships. Other honourable business associations are those of the Barclays and the Lloyds with banking, of Clarks with shoes, of Reckitts with starch, and of Allen & Hanburys with medicines. It should, moreover, be noticed that the Friends turned to business, as also to natural science, because careers in the Church, the armed forces, and

[1] The Fellowship of Reconciliation is, however, an interdenominational association of Christian Pacifists.

government services were closed to them. Amongst their most distinguished scientists are John Dalton and Joseph Lister in the nineteenth and Sir Arthur Eddington in the twentieth century. Their politicians and philanthropists include William Penn, Joseph Lancaster, Elizabeth Fry, John Woolman, John Bright, and Philip Noel-Baker, whilst their contribution to poetry is represented by John Greenleaf Whittier. If their numbers are few, their roll of honour indicates that they were astonishingly productive of leaders in different fields of life. If they are the leaven that leavens the lump, then the estimated world total of the members of the Society in 1940—163,000—may yet effect a transformation out of all proportion to their numbers. The father in God of this company of benefactors was George Fox.

Another man of the people was John Bunyan (1628–88), the son of a Bedfordshire tinsmith. He resembles Fox in his independence of mind, in the vividness of his imagination, in the direct simplicity of his writing and preaching, in his insistence upon experimental religion, and in his sufferings. It seems that a major factor in his conversion was, like that of Charles Wesley later, the reading of Martin Luther's Commentary on Galatians, in which he found his condition 'so largely and profoundly handled, as if his book had been written out of my heart'. Other factors were the influence of John Gifford, an Independent minister, and overhearing the religious conversation of certain poor Bedford women. His spiritual autobiography, *Grace Abounding*, informs us that he was set apart as a preacher by Gifford's congregation. When he was an itinerant evangelist hundreds came to hear his sermons, which were remarkable for their sincerity and passion. He attributed his success to these qualities. 'I preached

what I felt, what I did smartingly feel. . . . I have been
in my preaching . . . as if an angel of God had stood
by at my back to encourage me.' He spent the first
twelve years of the Restoration in gaol, keeping himself
by making laces, his library consisting only of the Bible
and Foxe's *Book of Martyrs*. During this period he
wrote *Grace Abounding*. Charles II's Declaration of
Indulgence of 1672 secured him only temporary relief,
and he was re-imprisoned in Bedford gaol on the bridge
over the Ouse in 1675. It was here that he wrote *The
Pilgrim's Progress*. The first part appeared in 1678, and
eleven editions were called for within ten years. By
1688 it had been translated into Dutch, French, and
Welsh. It depicts the journey of the Christian pilgrim
through this world to the world to come, and is the
most dynamic account of the Puritan conception of the
meaning of human life and destiny, whilst *The Holy
War* is the explanation of the ways of God to men, a
systematic exposition of Puritan theology, and the prose
equivalent of Milton's *Paradise Lost* and *Paradise
Regained*.

It is not difficult to account for the popularity of *The
Pilgrim's Progress* in an age when religious books formed
the only serious reading of humbler folk, for it mirrored
so dramatically the ideals, the feelings, and the struggles
of the common man. Moreover, the pill was most
attractively gilded so that the narrative pleased the
many and the inner meaning caused the meditative to
rejoice. Its greatness lies in the fact that it is, in Sir
Charles Firth's estimation, 'the prose epic of English
Puritanism'.[1] It represents Christianity not as a doctrinal system but as an enthralling and heroic way of
life, as it was for Nonconformists under the Clarendon

[1] *Essays Historical and Literary*, p. 172.

Code. The pilgrim turns his back on his home and his livelihood, and, setting his face towards the light, journeys towards the shining spires of the Celestial City. At every turn the world, the flesh, and the devil, not as bloodless abstractions, but as terrifying incarnations, essay to hinder and obstruct Christian's path. He is, indeed, *Christianus contra mundum*, the solitary soul struggling against the false values and meretricious pleasures of a vain world. It was the Baptist tinker's glory to 'weave a halo round the uncompromising and uncomfortable; and he raised a tribunal more solemn than any by which he was himself judged—that of human conscience'.[1] He waged relentless war not against evil as such, for every preacher and moralist has done that, but against the insidiousness of complacency. In his allegory a martyred Nonconformity recognized its greatness and, like Christian, encouraged companions in suffering:

I saw in my dream that Christian went not forth alone, for there was another whose name was Hopeful (being made so by the beholding of Christian and Faithful in their words and behaviour in their sufferings at the Fair) who joined himself unto him, and entering into a brotherly covenant, told him that he would be his companion.

Although inferior to Bunyan in vigour of conviction and imagination, Peter Sterry, Independency's representative in this period, had exactly the qualities that Bunyan lacked. Sterry (*d.* 1672) combined a Cavalier's upbringing and tastes with a Roundhead's religious convictions. He exhibited conspicuously the qualities of intellectual freedom, tolerance, loving-kindness, and

[1] Ogg, *op. cit.*, II, p. 740.

mental flexibility, and so uniquely as almost to constitute a new type of Puritanism. His natural mysticism
and belief that 'reason is the candle of the Lord' demonstrates the affinities of this former Fellow of Emmanuel
with the Cambridge Platonists. Unlike them, however,
he repudiated a 'cloistered virtue' and, as a member of
the Westminster Assembly and chaplain to the Protector, he bore 'the heat and burden of the day'. His
reading appears to have been more catholic than that of
any other Puritan of his time. His commonplace book
records the names of the volumes that he had with him
in Chelsea in 1663, and these included: St. Thomas's
Summa, the works of Cardinal Nicholas of Cusa, Ficino
the Italian Platonist, Savonarola the Florentine Reformer, Plotinus and Proclus the Neoplatonists, Seneca
and Bacon, Jacob Boehme the German mystic, the
Greek Father, Origen, and the works of Shakespeare,
Fletcher, and Ovid. He even possessed the French
romances *Le Grand Cyrus* and *Cassandra*. His friendships exhibited the same catholicity, for he was
acquainted with Milton and Marvell, was accepted as
the adopted son of Fulke Greville the statesman-poet,
and had many contacts with such leading Dissenting
divines as Owen and Goodwin, and with such of its
nobility as Lord Brook, and of the gentry as Sir Henry
Vane.

His toleration and independence of mind came to the
public knowledge in a sermon preached to the House of
Commons in November of 1645. Though this was the
time of the Parliamentary victory over the Royalists,
he spoke of the sufferings of his fellow-countrymen:
'Three Kingdoms stand before you this day, like those
three Crosses on Mount Golgotha, all laden with broken
and bleeding carkasses. These three doth your God

take, as one Text, that He may preach sin to your soules
from it, that He may convince you of sin by it.'[1] The
same independence of mind and courage of expression
led him to reject the tyranny of Rome and of Geneva,
which he described thus:

... the former is the Ghost of Judaisme cloathed
from the mantle which it wore in its life time, appearing
in the same outward pompe, with the same delicious
pleasures of Pictures, Musicke, Perfumes &c. as of old.
But the last is Judaism undrest, like an apparition in
chaines, or Lazarus when he came forth from the graves
with the grave-cloathes bound about him.[2]

He was an active member of Cromwell's inner circle
during the Protectorate, engaged in chaplaincy and
advisory duties, such as sitting on the committee that
recommended the re-admission of the Jews to England,
and that which was appointed to collect funds for the
distressed Waldenses in Piedmont; the Restoration
forced him into retirement, which he employed in the
writing of felicitous devotional treatises. His most celebrated work, *A Discourse of the Freedom of the Will*,
discloses in the title that he had cut the painter which
bound Independency to the quay of Calvinism. It also
exhibits, in an acrimonious age, a sustained plea for
toleration:

Some entertaining Strangers, have entertained Angels.
Do thou so believe, that in every encounter thou mayest
meet under the disguise of an Enemy, a Friend, a
Brother, who, when his Helmet shall be taken off, may
disclose a beautiful and a well-known face, which shall
charm all thy opposition into love and delight at the sight
of it.[3]

[1] Sermon, *The Spirit Convincing of Sinne.*
[2] V. de S. Pinto, *Peter Sterry Platonist and Puritan* (1934),
p. 171.   [3] *op. cit.*, p. 124.

His major theological work, *The Appearance of God to Man in the Gospel*, abounds in illuminating similes, as when describing the Fall, he writes: 'While we were Innocent, our Nakedness was our Purity, as a beautiful Face unveil'd, as a Jewel drawn from the Case. By the Fall we are naked, as a Sheep when his white Fleece is torn from him by the Briars; we are shamefully naked.'[1] In the same volume he pleads for an understanding with less of the severity of God and more of the Divine love:

Let not the Name of God be as a Cloud over your Heads, shadowing all about you; or as a dark Corner to Children, in which, they fear Bug-bears. This is that which we call God; *Pulcherrima rerum*, the best and greatest; the best of Beauties and Joys. The greatest in Sweetness and Love, as well as in Wisdom and Power. Such Thoughts of God should make you run often into his Arms, love to be familiar with him, and long to be like him. This is to be Holy.[2]

In many ways John Howe (1630–1705), the Presbyterian divine, resembles Sterry. A graduate of Christ's College, he was intimate with Henry More the Platonist, and became Fellow and Chaplain of Magdalen College, in the sister university of Oxford. He, too, was appointed domestic chaplain to Oliver Cromwell, and was ejected during the Restoration. Like Sterry he used his enforced leisure in writing, until he went to Antrim as Lord Massarene's domestic chaplain. He lived to see the 'glorious Revolution', and was a leading Presbyterian minister in the *rapprochement* with the Independents in 1690. He was intimate with great men, such as Richard Cromwell and William III. He also wrote an outstanding devotional work entitled *The Living Temple of God*, produced in 1675. It is 'a designed

[1] V. de S. Pinto, *op. cit.*, p. 233.   [2] *id.*, pp. 277–8.

improvement of that notion that a good man is the temple of God'. It is, in effect, a Puritan *Summa Theologiae*, for the first part consists of arguments for the existence of God derived from natural theology, and the second part is a demonstration that man fulfils his individual and communal relationships and needs through Jesus Christ, the Son of God. Its philosophical significance is considerable, since it is the first serious criticism of Deism. His irony had a sharp edge, as when he parodied the Deist creed in the words: 'There shall be a God, provided he be not meddlesome.' In a challenge to Stillingfleet's Sermon on Schism, he manifested an irenical spirit, claiming that 'without all controversy the main inlet of all the distractions, confusions and divisions of the Christian world hath been by adding other conditions of Church communion than Christ hath done'.[1] This shrewd judgement has lost none of its relevance to-day.

It was of Howe, Sterry, and their like, that Locke the philosopher wrote: 'Bartholomew Day was fatal to our Church and Religion, in throwing out a very great number of worthy, learned, pious, and orthodox divines who could not come up to some things in the Act of Uniformity.'[2] Despite, perhaps because of, their sufferings under the Clarendon Code, the Nonconformists faced the new century with a new confidence. They had won the right to be tolerated, even if they were still to suffer disabilities in position and civil rights. They made full use of their opportunities by taking out 2,418 licences for places of worship during the last twelve years of the century. On the accession of George I

[1] Works, v, p. 226.
[2] Locke's posthumous works, *Letter from a Person of Quality*.

in 1714, nearly a hundred of the English Dissenting ministers presented an address to the King. They wore grave Genevan gowns, and, as the dark procession moved towards the King, a nobleman touched the Independent Bradbury on the arm, and said, 'Pray, sir, what is this? A funeral?' 'No, my lord,' replied Bradbury, 'it is a Resurrection.'[1]

[1] Dale, *op. cit.*, p. 515.

CHAPTER VI

THE AGE OF TOLERATION

THE first three decades of the eighteenth century were marked by a growing expansion of the Dissenting Churches. New meeting-houses sprang up like mushrooms; Nonconformist religion ceased to be a hole-and-corner affair. The following table of places of worship registered after the *Toleration Act* indicates the new life that was pulsing amidst the Dissenters:[1]

				Temporary	Permanent
1688–90	.	.	.	796	143
1691–1700	.	.	.	1,247	32
1701–10	.	.	.	1,216	41
1711–20	.	.	.	862	21
1721–30	.	.	.	439	27
1731–40	.	.	.	418	21

Some of these buildings for worship reflected the impecuniousness of the congregations, rather than their taste in architecture. Others, like Dr. Taylor's octagonal Meeting-House in Norwich, reflected the growing wealth of the middle-classes in general, and of the merchants in particular. John Wesley writes of the latter:

I was shown Dr. Taylor's new meeting-house, perhaps the most elegant one in Europe. It is eight-square, built of the finest brick, with sixteen sash-windows below, as many above, and eight skylights in the dome; which, indeed, are purely ornamental. The inside is finished in

[1] Duncan Coomer, *English Dissent*, p. 61.

the highest taste, and is as clean as any nobleman's saloon. The communion-table is fine mahogany; the very latches of the pew-doors are polished brass. How can it be thought that the old, coarse Gospel should find admission here? [1]

In the middle of the century it is probably true, as Wesley suggests, that what the Dissenters gained in social respectability they lost in zeal; but this judgement would not hold good at the beginning of the century. However worldly-wise the Dissenting congregations in the middle of the century, requiring the rekindling of the flame on the altar of the heart by the ardent evangelist, the fires of Dissenting devotion burned steadily and clear at the commencement of the century, the age of Isaac Watts and Philip Doddridge.

The honour for the composition of the first modern hymn must go to a Baptist, Benjamin Keach, pastor of the Church at Horsleydown. His verses, though they did not break the laws of God, broke the laws of metre. It is to Isaac Watts that the Free Churches owe a double debt: he gave the people of God the right to sing in soaring verse the glories of their God, after they had been filched from them by trained choirs, and he reformed the prayers of the pastors, by urging them to refrain from dependence on 'sudden motions' for *ex tempore* worship.

Watts departed from the literalism of the older versions of the Psalms, claiming 'In all places I have kept my grand design in view; and that is to teach my author to speak like a Christian.' [2] He reduced the original Psalms to a suitable length for singing, and avoided bold metaphors and Biblical obscurities, in the

---

[1] *Journal*, entry for Nov. 23, 1757.
[2] Watts, *Opera*, IV, p. 119.

cause of intelligibility and interest. Some of his para-
phrases were imperishable, the more illustrious of them
being: the 72nd ('Jesus shall reign where e'er the sun'),
the 92nd ('Sweet is the work my God and King'), the
117th ('From all that dwell below the skies'), the 122nd
('How pleas'd and blest was I'), and the 146th ('I'll
praise my Maker with my breath'). His finest paraphrase, the 90th ('Our God, our help in ages past'), has
become a favourite on solemn national occasions in
England. The measure of his achievement may be seen
by a comparison of his work with that of his pre-
decessors. John Patrick, in his *Psalms of David in
Metre*, paraphrased the 90th Psalm thus:

> Our age to seventy years are set,
> If to another stage we get,
> And unto fourscore years arrive,
> We rather sigh and groan than live.

In Watts this common versification takes on a kingly
tread:

> Time, like an ever-rolling stream,
> Bears all its sons away;
> They fly forgotten as a dream
> Dies at the opening day.

It was left for Watts to make the daring transition from
a free paraphrase to a Christian hymn. This he achieved
in his *Hymns and Spiritual Songs*, which included such
masterpieces as: 'Awake our souls, away our fears',
'Come let us join our cheerful songs', 'I'm not ashamed
to own my Lord', 'Join all the glorious names', 'There
is a land of pure delight', 'Give me the wings of faith
to rise', and the magnificent 'When I survey the won-
drous Cross'. His claim to distinction is that he taught
the Puritans to sing their creed in his metrical orthodox

I

confessions of faith. That, whilst the Presbyterians
withered away in Arianism, the Congregationalists remained staunchly orthodox must be, in a large measure,
attributed to Watts.

A pioneer in praises, Watts was also a reformer of
prayers. Matthew Henry wrote in 1710:

> And it is requisite to the decent Performance of the
> Duty, that some proper Method be observ'd, not only
> that what is said be good, but that it be said in its proper
> Place and Time; and that we offer not anything to the
> Glorious Majesty of Heaven and Earth, which is con-
> fus'd, impertinent, and indigested.[1]

Watts addressed himself to this problem in the *Guide
to Prayer* of 1716. His noble conception of prayer is
made clear in his fine definition of it as 'that converse
which God hath allowed us to maintain with Himself
above, while we are here below. It is that language
wherein the creature holds correspondence with his
Creator; and wherein the soul gets near to God, is
entertained with great delight, and, as it were, dwells
with his Heavenly Father for a short season before
he comes to heaven.' He provides a mnemonic for
the parts of prayer, that indicates his wide scope of
treatment:

> Call upon God, adore, confess,
> Petition, plead, and then declare
> You are the Lord's, give thanks and bless,
> And let Amen confirm the prayer.

To depart from such an order in prayer is like fulfilling
all our errands at once, he declares. He then ridicules
improper diction in prayer. Instances that merit his
criticism are then given. 'Thou, O Lord, art our *dernier*

---

[1] Matthew Henry, *A Method of Prayer*, p. A4 *recto*.

resort' is unsuitable because foreign diction; 'we do
Thee to wit' is derided as obsolete; and he condemns
such philosophical expressions as the following: 'Thou
art hypostatically three, and essentially one; by the
plentitude of perfection in Thine own essence, Thou
art self-sufficient for Thine own existence.' If Watts
had had his way, he would have persuaded the Independents to relinquish the 'Congregational crouch' as a
posture of prayer, for he says: 'And in this case it is
very proper to conform to the usage of Christians with
whom we worship, whether standing or kneeling. . . .'
Whilst he values set forms of prayer, he complains that
'generals are cold and do not affect us, nor affect persons
that join with us'. But these he would prefer to *ex
tempore* effusions that result from 'an entire dependence
on sudden motions and suggestions'. He knew, however, that without the blessing of God even the best of
rules would be valueless, 'but a fair carcass without a
soul'. Watts is a proof, if any were needed, that God
did not leave Himself without a witness even in the
aridity of the early eighteenth century. A distinguished
philosopher and theologian, a pioneer in education, he
was supremely the Christian poet. Honoured in his life
by the honorary Doctorate of Divinity of the University
of Edinburgh, he was honoured in his burial in Westminster Abbey and by inclusion in Johnson's *Lives of
the Poets.*

A name of almost equal greatness is that of Philip
Doddridge, friend and follower of Watts. Whilst many
of Doddridge's hymns are too didactic, because he
framed them upon the substance of his sermons to be
sung by his congregation, line by line, whilst his doctrine was fresh in their memory, others have passed
the test of time. Among the most famous are: 'Hark

the glad sound, the Saviour comes', 'Ye servants of the Lord', 'Lord of the Sabbath, hear our vows', and the great sacramental hymn 'My God, and is Thy Table spread?' His Academy at Northampton was one of the outstanding educational institutions of the age, for the curriculum included modern subjects not as yet taught in either of the ancient universities. During the four years' course, his pupils studied the ancient languages (Greek, Latin, and Hebrew); a modern language (French); such modern subjects as Geography, History (English and Civil and Jewish Antiquities), and Architecture; such science subjects as Physics, Mechanics, Hydrostatics, Astronomy, Globes, Geometry, Algebra, and Anatomy; and philosophical subjects such as Logic and Ethics. Practical training was given in Oratory and 'Critics and Controversies.' All in all, this was as liberal an education as could be obtained in eighteenth-century England.

The chief debt, however, which the Free Churches owe to Doddridge is for a remarkable essay in personal religion, entitled *The Rise and Progress of Religion in the Soul.* This volume, produced in 1744, not only revived the waning devotion of the Nonconformists, but was a major influence on William Carey, the founder of the modern missionary movement in the Protestant Churches, which was to take the Gospel to the ends of the globe, and to make Protestantism a world-force. This is Free Church religion at its finest, devout and scholarly, humble and practical. Doddridge says in the Preface that there are two types of Christian, the 'once-born' and the 'twice-born', but his volume is only for the latter. His definition of religion is admirable: 'Religion, in its most general view, is such a sense of God on the soul, and such a conviction of our obligation to Him, and of our dependence upon Him, as shall engage us to make it our great care, to conduct ourselves in a manner well-pleasing . . . to Him.'[1] He plans the book for the man and the Christian in a variety of circumstances. The first ten chapters are aimed at the case of the thoughtless and apathetic by convicting them of guilt and 'the dreadful sentence of the righteous and Almighty God', leading to the proclamation of the Gospel of forgiveness. Then he turns to the case of a soul overwhelmed by its sense of sin and unable to believe in forgiveness. He shows the signs of true repentance and faith, and exhibits vividly the characteristics of the Christian life, and the ways in which the Christian may receive the assistance of the Holy Spirit (Chapters XI to XVI). His third section is devoted to the young convert, to steel him against discouragements and difficulties, and to explain the means of grace and prescribe a regimen for the devotional life and to caution against various temptations. Fourthly, he addresses himself to Christians undergoing a period of dryness in their spiritual life, uncovering the causes of their declension and apostasy, and considering the Christian when 'under hidings of God's face' and when 'struggling under great and heavy afflictions'. His fifth section aims at assisting the zealous Christian to assess his growth in grace from increasing love of God to 'habitual and cheerful willingness to exchange worlds whenever God shall appoint it'. He then exhorts the advanced Christian to remember the love and mercy of God towards him by regular spiritual exercises. He ends by preparing the Christian for death and judgement, beseeching him to 'honour God by his dying behaviour'.

[1] *op. cit.*, Chapter I.

Even a brief summary will indicate the wide scope and practical value of a book which was to serve the Nonconformists throughout the century as St. Ignatius Loyola's *Spiritual Exercises* stiffened the devotion and discipline of the Jesuits. This devotional classic of the eighteenth century was pre-eminent in three respects. First, for the simple directness of its approach, 'I shall here speak in a looser and freer manner, as a friend to a friend; just as I would do, if I were to be in person admitted to a private audience, by one whom I tenderly loved, and whose circumstance and character I knew to be like that which the title of one chapter or another of this treatise describes.' Secondly, it provides a combination of practical advice with suitable prayers: 'And when I have discoursed with him a little while, which will seldom be so long as half an hour, I shall, as it were, step aside and leave him to meditate on what he has heard, or endeavour to assist him in such fervent addresses to God as it may be proper to mingle with these meditations.' Its third merit is the psychological approach, recognizing the differing states and needs of the Christian, young or mature, lethargic or oversensitive to sin, in temptations, under afflictions, or facing death.

The outstanding contribution made in this century to the religion of the Free Churches (and, indeed, to the entire religious life of England), was the Evangelical Revival spread by the zeal and organizing genius of the Methodists, the youngest, and in many ways the most vigorous, of the English Free Churches. However, to imply that Puritanism was dead, and the Nonconformists in a dull torpor, is to dishonour the memory of many who continued honourably to defend the evangelical fort, beleaguered by the attacks of Deism and Arianism, the disdain for enthusiasm in the Augustan age, and the prevalent contempt for religion and morality. Methodism's greatness cannot be increased, by diminishing the fidelity of the few evangelical ministers of the older Dissenting Churches in England.

It is, it should be admitted, scarcely possible to exaggerate the moral and spiritual paralysis which had brought religion almost to its death-bed in the England of the mid-eighteenth century. Inevitably Methodism seemed like a resurrection of a Church in whose body *rigor mortis* had set in. If the situation was serious in the Established Church and amongst the Dissenters, it was incredibly dark in the general social life of the nation.

The degenerate profligacy of the courtiers was matched by the callous economic orgies of the tradesmen who abounded in a 'nation of shopkeepers'. Statesmen and leaders of society were not ashamed to appear inebriated. Robert Walpole, for instance, sat with his father for a nightly carouse, and the father poured a double draught for the son, saying: 'Come Robert, you shall drink twice to my once, for I will not permit the son in his sober senses to be witness of his father's intoxication'. Lord Chesterfield, the arbiter of fashion, thought it prudent to instruct his young son in 'The art of seduction as part of a polite education'. Hogarth's cartoons turned the social satirist's spotlight on to the debauchery and squalid sluttery of London's poor, where every sixth house was a liquor saloon. Even the savagery of the laws (and the death penalty applied to no fewer than 160 offences) failed utterly to restrain the licentiousness and dishonesty of the times. The English people, according to Hume, had settled 'into the most cool indifference with regard to religious matters that is to be found in any nation in the world'.

Even the supporters of religion were in a sorry plight. The successors of the Puritans were largely discredited amongst thinking persons, because of their association in the common mind with the fantastic sectaries of the Commonwealth. After the Exeter controversy, many of the younger Presbyterian ministers openly denied the divinity of Jesus Christ, and seceded to Arianism, their sermons degenerating into philosophical discourses or moral disquisitions.[1] The Establishment fought a long and continuing battle with Deism, which was to make its religious emphasis over-intellectualistic, even when it safeguarded orthodoxy. The Deists rested their arguments on three foundations: that natural religion, not revealed, is universally binding; that such natural religion alone gives hope for honourable men who stood outside the Christian revelation; and that priestcraft has corrupted primitive truth. Acceptance of Deism in the interests of a supposedly rational religion had devastating effects on the religious understanding of men. They deprecated all ardour and sacrifice in the cause of Christ as 'mere enthusiasm', and the distinctive doctrines of Christianity (the Trinity and the Incarnation, for example) as unintelligent accretions to a simple belief in the Fatherhood of God and the brotherhood of men. So deeply had Deism corroded the fabric of orthodox Churchmanship that its most doughty opponent, Bishop Butler of Bristol, informed John Wesley in 1739 that 'faith itself is a good work; it is a virtuous temper of mind'. Then, lest Wesley should misunderstand that morality and religion meant

[1] See J. Black, *Presbyterianism in England in the Eighteenth and Nineteenth Centuries* (1887), pp. 15–20.

the same thing, he added: 'Sir, the pretending to extra-
ordinary revelations and gifts of the Holy Ghost is a
horrid thing—a very horrid thing. You have no business here; you are not commissioned to preach in this
diocese. I therefore advise you to go hence.'[1] And, be
it remembered, these words came from one who complained in his *Analogy* that 'it has come to be taken for
granted that Christianity is not so much a subject for
inquiry, but that it is now discovered to be fictitious'.
Christian discipleship and sacrifice were now regarded
as undisguised fanaticism. Swift, in his *Argument
against abolishing Christianity*, defends the Churches
in the following ironical statement: 'Where are more
appointments and rendezvous of gallantry? Where are
more meetings for business? Where more bargains
driven of all sorts? And where so many conveniences
and incitements to sleep?' In short, where religion was
not formal, it was rational, and where it was not rational,
it was merely moral.

Whitefield and the Wesleys were to revive religion in
England by taking the Gospel to the people, to improve
the moral and social conditions of industrial England
out of all recognition, and to fan the flame that burst
into modern missionary ardour. It may well be, as
Élie Halévy insisted, that the evangelization of the
masses by the Methodists prevented England's prole-
tariat from emulating the French Revolution of 1789.

There were four outstanding figures in the Evangelical Revival: John Wesley its director and supreme
organizer, also outstanding as a preacher; Charles
Wesley its poet; George Whitefield its prince of
preachers and most fertile of experimenters in religion;
and its saint, Fletcher of Madeley, unconspicuous as a

[1] Wesley, *Journal*, entry for 1739.

saint should be. John Wesley towered above the rest, combining a profound evangelical passion with a genius for administration. 'In John Wesley', says B. L. Manning, 'the Methodists had a leader who, by a stroke of divine genius that puts him in the same rank as Hildebrand, St. Dominic, and St. Ignatius Loyola, combined the evangelical passion and experience of Luther with Calvin's ecclesiastical system.'[1]

Wesley's conversion is a commonplace of the history books, but it is insufficiently realized that it transformed a meticulous High Churchman and a Tory into a flaming emissary of the living God.[2] That he had been released from bondage to the Law into Christian freedom is shown by the four resolutions he entered into his Journal for 28 February 1738, barely three months before his liberating experience in Aldersgate Street:

1. To use absolute openness and unreserve with all I should converse with;
2. To labour after continual seriousness, not willingly indulging myself in any the least levity of behaviour, or in laughter; no, not for a moment;
3. To speak no word which does not tend to the glory of God; in particular, not to talk of worldly things. Others may, nay, must. But what is that to thee? And,
4. To take no pleasure which does not tend to the glory of God; thanking God every moment for all I do take, and therefore rejecting every sort and degree of it which I feel I cannot so thank Him in and for.

How negative, stilted, and inhibited he was, how scrupulous and humourless, before his conversion.

[1] *The Making of Modern English Religion*, p. 110.
[2] Cf. K. S. Latourette, *A History of the Expansion of Christianity*, VII, p. 490.

How different from the entry of 5 June 1739! This reads:

I look upon all the world as my parish; thus far I mean, that, in whatever part of it I am, I judge it meet, right and my bounden duty, to declare unto all that are willing to hear, the glad tidings of salvation.

This is the Wesley who throws down the gauntlet to the whole bench of bishops, with statesmanlike vision as wide as the earth itself. This Mr. Valiant-for-truth contested the three kingdoms for the cause of Christ in a tireless campaign that lasted for forty years. It was accomplished on horse-back, with the saddle as his only study. From the entry in his diary for 28 June 1774, where he claims that his minimum mileage for each year was 4,500, we may compute that in the course of his ministry he travelled 225,000 miles; that is, almost ten times round the world. Moreover, in each year he preached about 5,000 sermons. He and his devout Methodist preachers were the first preachers since the Franciscan friars to bring the Gospel to the working-classes. This he accomplished despite a jealous wife, suits in chancery, the envious opposition of the clergy of the Established Church, and the furious assaults of enraged mobs.

This unconventional ambassador of God used a pulpit wherever he could find one. It might be the natural amphitheatre of Gwennap in Cornwall, where he preached to over 30,000 souls at once, or his father's tombstone in Epworth churchyard, when refused admission to the church. He would proclaim the good news in village squares and in city streets, on rocks and on quaysides, on mountain-tops like the Calton Hill in Edinburgh, or inside houses where the windows were left wide open so that the great overflow of worshippers outside might hear.

This was no ordinary revival, a mere upthrust of emotionalism, as its results were to show. Wesley himself wrote in 1739:

> I will show you him that was a lion until then and is now a lamb; him that was a drunkard and is now exemplarily sober; the whoremonger that was who now abhors the very 'garment spotted by the flesh'. These are my living arguments for what I assert, viz. That God does now, as aforetime, give remission of sins, and the gift of the Holy Spirit even to us and to our children— yea, and suddenly, as far as I have known, in dreams and visions of God.

Part of his genius lay in his pragmatism. He confessed that he would, at one time, have 'thought the saving of souls almost a sin if it had not been done in Church', but seeing the amazing conversions effected by Whitefield, he withdrew his objections, and became himself an enthusiastic field-preacher. In the same way, he once had a violent antipathy to laymen preaching, and was only dissuaded from stopping Thomas Maxfield preaching in London, by the rebuke of his mother. Yet so well had he learnt this lesson that he could write to Alexander Mather: 'Give me one hundred preachers who fear nothing but sin, and desire nothing but God, and I care not a straw whether they be clergymen or laymen, such alone will shake the gates of Hell, and set up the kingdom of heaven upon earth.' He had besought the Bishop of London on two occasions to ordain Methodist preachers for North America, and, the request being refused, he had no scruples in setting apart Whatcoat and Vasey as presbyters, and Dr. Coke as superintendent for the American Society.

Charles Wesley's timid spirit expressed itself in the squib:

> How easily are bishops made
> By man or woman's whim!
> Wesley his hand on Coke hath laid,
> But who laid hands on him?

His administrative ability was seen alike in the formation of Methodist Societies up and down the country, in the organization of the Christian Library for the assistance of his local preachers, and in the orphanage he set up in Newcastle, and the schools at Kingswood. For a rigorous High Churchman to take to field-preaching, to train lay preachers and ordain some of them, and to encourage extemporary prayers, was a signal proof of adaptability.

What, then, were the forces that went into the making of this remarkable apostle of the eighteenth century? Strenuous self-discipline, as evinced by the regimen of the Holy Club days; the courage of his own convictions, inherited, it may be, from his persecuted Nonconformist ancestors on both sides of the family; the influence of a brilliant and godly mother, such as Susannah Wesley was; a classical training that opened the New Testament to him in the original tongue and trained him in scholarly habits. But we have not yet penetrated to the springs of his devotion. There was an early experience of being marvellously rescued when the Epworth Rectory was ablaze that gave him a sense of being 'a brand plucked from the burning', a consecrated spirit. There was wide and deep reading in the mystics: the *Theologica Germanica*, Tauler, Macarius, Madam Guyon, Brother Lawrence, Pascal, the Cambridge Platonists, William Law, and Molinos. These were his

spiritual directors, but it was the most protestant of
Protestants, Martin Luther, who claimed his soul's
most passionate ardour for Christ. On the red-letter
day of the Methodist calendar (24 May 1738) we read
the entry in his Journal:

> In the evening I went very unwillingly to a society in
> Aldersgate Street, where one was reading Luther's Pre-
> face to the Epistle to the Romans. About a quarter before
> nine, while he was describing the change which God
> works in the heart through faith in Christ, I felt my heart
> strangely warmed. I felt I did trust in Christ, Christ
> alone, for salvation; and an assurance was given me that
> He had taken away my sins, even mine, and saved me
> from the law of sin and death.

The world's great Reformers have been in the authentic
Pauline succession. It was the Epistle to the Romans
that captured St. Augustine in the Milan garden, that
gave Luther, as he lectured in Wittenberg, freedom
from the thraldom of justification by works, and, in our
own time, seized the soul of Dr. Karl Barth. It was to
captivate John Wesley. There is no more passionate
theological formulation of the Gospel, and Luther is an
admirable exponent of St. Paul. As Coleridge said:
'The only fit commentator on St. Paul was Luther—
not by any means such a gentleman, but almost as great
a genius.' Charles Wesley, it is of interest to record,
was converted as a result of reading Luther's Commentary on the Epistle to the Galatians. The common
factor in each case was the Moravian brethren, who
honoured Luther, and introduced the Wesley brothers
to his writings.

Charles Wesley, it has been remarked, was the poet of
the Revival. He was more; he was its most popular theologian, for his hymns were the creed of the Methodists.

Of the first Methodist hymn-book, B. L. Manning declares: 'This little book ranks in Christian literature with the Psalms, the Book of Common Prayer, the Canon of the Mass.'[1] The same historian on the same theme declares that the merits of Wesley's hymns are threefold: 'There is the solid structure of historic dogma; there is the passionate thrill of present experience; but there is, too, the glory of a mystic sunlight coming from another world.'[2] These hymns record every mood of the soul, and supremely the daring confidence of faith. They recapture the radiance of the New Testament itself. They belong not to one church, but to the whole of English-speaking Christendom.

There are hymns provided by Charles Wesley for all the great Christian festivals: for Christmas 'Hark! the herald angels sing', for Easter 'Christ the Lord is risen to-day', for Ascensiontide 'Hail the day that sees Him rise', for Whitsuntide 'Granted is the Saviour's prayer', for Trinity Sunday 'Hail! Holy, Holy, Holy Lord', for missionary celebrations 'Eternal Lord of earth and skies', for dedication 'Forth in Thy name, O Lord, I go', and for the Eucharist 'Victim Divine, Thy grace we claim'. No greater religious poet has put himself so completely at the service of the Church. On his winged words Methodism sang its way into the hearts of the common people.

What, we may ask, was the theology which inspired the songs of Charles and the sermons of John Wesley? With the Reformers it derived its inspiration from the Bible, but it went behind the Bible to the mighty acts of God in revelation, as they were confirmed in personal experience. No Methodist was content to know God

[1] *The Hymns of Wesley and Watts*, p. 14.
[2] *op. cit.*, p. 29.

at second-hand. In the second place, it sounded the
death-knell of Calvinism and the doctrine of double pre-
destination in the interests of free grace and universal
salvation:

> Throughout the world its breadth is known,
>   Wide as infinity;
> So wide it never passed by one,
>   Or had it passed by me.

So far this was a recovery, rather than a discovery, of
the gospel of Luther, justification by faith and the joyful
assurance of the forgiveness of sins. The third mark of
the Methodist theology was more distinctive: a profound emphasis on the doctrine of sanctification, and a
new exposition of it. John Wesley believed in 'Christian
perfection'. Whilst accused frequently of hypocrisy in
holding the doctrine, Wesley insisted that it took
seriously our Lord's command 'Be ye perfect . . .' and
refused to admit the possibility of the defeat of God's
love. Salvation became, not a future event or state, but
a present fact. It was not the imposition of a galling
disciplinary yoke, but the discovery of joyous freedom.
Moreover, the saved individual joined himself to others
to form a worshipping, witnessing, redeeming community. The two most striking notes of Methodist
faith and life are a first-hand experience of the re-
demptive love of Christ, and the urge to fellowship.

The finest preacher in the Revival was a Calvinist,
George Whitefield. It is clear that he was gifted with a
resonant voice and a vivid imagination. On his first
voyage to North America in 1736, it is recorded that
when the two smaller vessels came close to the *Whitaker*
(Whitefield's ship), Whitefield would preach to the
companies of the three ships, his great voice being

heard above the roaring surge of the ocean. Lord Chesterfield, it is said, once heard him describe a blind old man, deserted by his dog, stumbling on the brink of a steep cliff. This so stirred the ignoble Lord's imagination that, when the catastrophe approached, he cried out in an agonized tone, 'Good God, he is gone!' Hume thought it worth while going twenty miles to hear him preach. The famous philosopher gives the following as an example of the preacher's dramatic perorations:

Once, after a solemn pause, he thus addressed his audience:—'The attendant angel is just about to leave the threshold of this sanctuary and ascend to heaven. And shall he ascend and not bear with him the news of one sinner among all this multitude reclaimed from the error of his way?' Then he stamped with his foot, lifted up his hands and eyes to heaven, and cried aloud, 'Stop, Gabriel! stop ere you enter the sacred portals, and yet carry with you the news of one sinner converted to God!'[1]

Sponsored by Selina, Countess of Huntingdon, Whitefield made her salon a popular preaching venue. He appealed alike to nobility and the peasantry. He was as much at home when in the drawing-rooms of the aristocratic, as when the miners of Kingswood shed tears that ran like white rivers down their black cheeks, or when he was pelted with missiles by an abusive crowd at a fair-ground.

He was not only a powerful preacher, but the path-breaker for Methodism. He was the first to experience the evangelical conversion. He was the pioneer of open-air and field-preaching as he was the first to realize the

[1] Cited in Abbey and Overton, *The English Church in the Eighteenth Century*, II, p. 95.

K

potentialities of the Religious Societies of the period, which provided the model for the Methodist Societies. He first saw the necessity for lay preachers, and appointed them. He it was who first entered the field of religious journalism. He first carried the Evangelical Revival to Scotland, Ireland, and the colonies in North America. Whitefield was a pioneer philanthropist, building an orphanage of great size in North America. His contribution to the furtherance of education is greatly in advance of that of Wesley. He furthered the progress of the Methodist school at Kingswood and the Northampton Academy of Dr. Doddridge. In North America he furthered the work of Harvard College, Dartmouth College, and Mr. Wheelock's College for Indians. He encouraged the growth of the Log College, afterwards moved to Princeton, and the mother of Princeton University, whilst his charity school at Philadelphia grew into the University of Pennsylvania. He was responsible for founding the Churches known as the Countess of Huntingdon's Connexion, later united with the Congregational Union. In America he brought into existence more than a hundred and fifty Congregational Churches in twenty years. He revived many dying Presbyterian Churches in the same country, and was mainly responsible for the foundation of the Calvinistic Methodists who have played so large a part in the life of Wales. His contribution and his spirit were ecumenical.

The fourth, though the least conspicuous, of the Methodist giants was the saint, Fletcher of Madeley. He spent twenty-five years in this large Shropshire village, beloved by all who knew him. He had a remarkable capacity for divining the supernatural in the natural, and even in the commonplace. He was, in fact, the George Herbert of the Methodists. When he was, on one occasion, having his likeness taken, he exhorted 'the limner and all that were in the room, not only to get the outlines drawn, but the colourings also of the image of Jesus in their hearts'. When the surgeon ordered a blood-letting, whilst the blood was actually running into the cup, he took occasion 'to expatiate on the precious blood-shedding of the Lamb of God'. He used to tell the cook 'to stir up the fire of Divine love in her soul' and the chambermaid 'to sweep every corner in her heart'.

What was intended to be revival within the Church, was forced out of the Establishment through lack of sympathy. Thus Wesley, a loyal son of the Church of England, became a separatist against his will. The reasons for the antagonism on the part of the Establishment are not far to seek. The rational and moral character of the prevailing emphases in religion was inimical to enthusiasm in any form. Wesley and his followers were suspected at once of the extremes of Puritanism and sacerdotalism. Some of his preachers renounced both reason and scholarship, though the majority were taught to welcome both by Wesley himself. The chief stones of stumbling were, however, the irregularities in church order practised by Wesley. These were: field-preaching, the use of *extempore* prayers in preference to set forms, the appointment of lay preachers, the establishment of Societies, Synods, and Conferences, and, the final rock of offence, the ordination of the preachers for North America. To Wesley's credit it must be said that he hesitated until he could wait no longer. The Church had been given many opportunities to welcome Methodism, but she closed the door to every approach. But for Wesley's loyalty to the Church of which he was a priest, the inevitable rupture would have occurred earlier. Moreover, these irregularities are the reasons for the success of Methodism as a church polity; to have yielded them up at the behest of an authoritative Church would have been to fly in the face of God's manifest blessings.

In conclusion, we must turn to the permanent effects of the Methodist Revival. On 16 June 1755 John Wesley reviewed the success of his work in the following words:

> From the deep sense of the amazing work which God has of late years wrought in England, preached in the evening on these words (Psalm cxlvii. 20) 'He hath not dealt so with any nation.' . . . This must appear to all who impartially consider, 1. The numbers of persons on whom God has wrought; 2. The swiftness of His work in many, both convinced and truly converted in a few days; 3. The depth of it in most of these, changing the heart, as well as the whole conversation; 4. The clearness of it, enabling them boldly to say, 'Thou hast loved me; Thou hast given Thyself for me'; 5. The continuance of it.

The first fact, and the most telling, is corroborated by statistics of Methodist membership. In 1791, the year of Wesley's death, there were 71,688 members in Great Britain, 5,300 members in Foreign Societies, and 42,265 members in North America, making a total of 119,253 Methodist members. There were, in 1949, 750,612 Methodist members in Great Britain, and 10,169,125 in the United States of America, with a world total of 11,666,646 Methodists.[1] The numbers of souls converted by Whitefield cannot now be

[1] Grubb and Bingle (ed:), *World Christian Handbook* (1949), p. 240.

computed, since they joined the Anglican, Presbyterian, and Congregational Churches, not to mention the strong growth of the Calvinistic Methodist Churches in Wales. Suffice it to say that a tidal wave of religion swept over England, the like of which had not been seen since the days of the Reformation, if then.

It was to provide a vigorous experiential theology and a profound sense of fellowship; it was to open the eyes of Protestants to their world-wide responsibilities and to revitalize all the Churches in England as they followed the lead of the Baptists in founding their own foreign missionary societies; it was to assist in the transformation of the social life of the country in the philanthropic endeavours of the succeeding century; it was to reach the working-classes and to train them in the fundamentals of democracy as they exercised responsibility for the government of the Church and learned the art of public-speaking in making their testimonies; it was to put all Christendom in its debt for hymns which make orthodoxy enchanting and are the common man's theological primer; its Sunday Schools, which had in fact preceded the establishment of those founded by Robert Raikes, were to provide an elementary education long before the State recognized its responsibilities for educating the underprivileged. All these were, however, the by-products of the Movement. Its heart was the desire of one loving soul to set another afire with love of Christ. Close as the affinities of Methodism appear to be with Anglicanism, its evangelical passion and experiential religion were a revival of Puritan religion, without the latter's austerities and asperities. Its deepest affinities lie with the older Nonconformist Churches, for all are united in claiming that the Church is the servant of the Gospel, not the Gospel the servant of the Church. 'Puritanism', says J. R. Green, 'won its spiritual victory in the Wesleyan Movement, after the failure in the previous century of its military and political struggles.'[1]

[1] *Short History of the English People*, pp. 307–8.

CHAPTER VII

THE ERA OF EXPANSION

A BARELY tolerated and almost dying Dissent in the eighteenth century was resuscitated by the Evangelical Revival, thus preparing for the nineteenth century as an age of renewed advance. The effects of the Methodist Revival were to be seen not only in the growing influence and numbers of the Wesleyan Methodists and the Countess of Huntingdon's Connexion, but in the new shoots that now proliferated from the Puritan trunk in a second spring for the Baptist and Congregational Churches and for the 'Low' or Evangelical party of the Anglican Church, which was to be closely associated with the Free Churches in widespread philanthropic movements during the century. All dissenting denominations, except the Socinian Presbyterians, benefited from this remarkable religious awakening. Religious meetings multiplied; half-empty churches were filled again to overflowing. In many churches an additional evening service of a more popular character declared that churchmen now sought to 'catch the sinners, rather than to coddle the saints'.[1] Early Sunday morning prayer-meetings became the rule rather than the exception. New academies, as at Newport Pagnell, sprang up in which evangelical ordinands for the Established and Free Churches were trained side by side. Sunday Schools, founded by Robert Raikes of Gloucester in 1783, an adjunct to the work of the Church of England, were paid the flattery of

[1] A characteristic phrase coined by Hugh Price Hughes.

Nonconformist imitation. Clearly the tide of Augustan scepticism or apathy had turned; and religious revival brought in its wake a renewed social consciousness, for John Howard, the prison reformer, was proving that the Epistle of St. James had a message, as well as the Epistles of St. Paul.

The new century was, however, more than the rakish eighteenth century reformed; it had its own distinctive characteristics that represented advances in the life of the Free Churches. In general, its character was marked by six traits. It was for the Nonconformists a time of struggle first for religious liberty and then for religious equality with the Church of England. It was also an era remarkable for educational and social philanthropy. In the third place, it was a period in which denominations divided (notably in the case of the Methodists) and sects proliferated. It also saw the expansion of Protestant world missions, itself partly the fruit of the Evangelical Awakening of 1859 and after.[1] It was the age of the Nonconformist Conscience, formed largely by the means of great personalities and fearless preachers. Lastly, it was during the Victorian age that the new science came to blows with the old religion and caused much heart-searching, though the careful listener could have heard the rumbles of the approaching storm in the last decades of the preceding century. In view of the growing influence, both religious, social, and intellectual, of the Free Churches this chapter may not inaptly be named 'The Era of Expansion'.

The struggle for the recognition of the place of the Free Churches in English religious life is marked by two stages. The first consists of various attempts to

[1] cf. J. E. Orr, *The Second Evangelical Awakening in Britain* (1949).

repeal discriminatory legislation that disabled the Non-conformists; the second stage is characterized by a desire to attain to religious and social equality with the Establishment. The battle was joined when the Anglican protagonist, Lord Sidmouth, gave notice in 1808 of a Bill to withdraw the licences for Nonconformist meeting-houses issued during the previous thirty years. In retaliation, the Dissenters founded 'The Protestant Society for the Protection of Religious Liberty' which, with the assistance of the Dissenting Deputies, resolved on a vigorous campaign for the repeal of the Five Mile and Conventicle Acts. By 1812, when Castlereagh espoused the cause, a Parliamentary proposal for repeal of the Acts aroused practically no opposition. However, only the first campaign had been won, and there were further battles in store. The next objective of the Nonconformists was the repeal of the Test and Corporation Acts, with their grave civil disabilities for non-Anglicans. Lord John Russell proposed their deletion from the Statute Book in 1828, and the Government, under the Duke of Wellington, surprised that the Bill of repeal had a majority of forty-four on the first division, dropped its opposition. Thus within thirty years of the opening of the century all *direct* penalties for Nonconformity were abolished; only the indirect penalties remained. This victory may be attributed to several factors, amongst them the growth of the secular spirit of toleration as a result of the French and American Revolutions of the previous century, the numerical increase of Nonconformist members and adherents in the newer industrial towns, and the respect in which Nonconformists were held as supporters of law and order amongst strata of society hitherto antinomian or subversive.

The second stage of the Nonconformist struggle was entered with the aim of removing the minor disabilities from which they still suffered. The ancient national universities would open their doors only to subscribers to the thirty-nine Articles, with the result that able Dissenters had either to send their sons away to the four Scottish universities, or assist in the establishment of modern, unsectarian universities, until such time as the barriers should fall. Also, believing that the Church of England was tantamount to a branch of the Civil Service, and owing their very *raison d'être* to the fact that they were *Free* Churches, they were compelled to subsidize what they abhorred, by the payment of church rates for the support of the Establishment. Furthermore, they could not have their children's births registered unless they went to the local incumbent for christening; their marriages were only legally valid if performed in an Anglican church, and they had to be buried according to the rites of the Book of Common Prayer. Moreover, insult was added to injury in the opprobrium hurled at the Dissenters as Jacobins, sinister revolutionaries, cloaking their fell designs against Church and State with religion. Inevitably, this struggle for equality embittered relationships between the Anglican and Free Churches during the century, though a happier spirit prevailed in the joint philanthropic enterprises undertaken by evangelicals within and outside the Establishment. In time the Free Churches, under the pressure of increasing vexations, came to believe that their only hope of equality lay in the Disestablishment of the Church of England. In 1844 the British Anti-State-Church Society was founded, and later renamed the Liberation Society. The leading exponents of this root-and-branch policy were Dr. R. W. Dale of Birmingham and Edward Miall, the editor of *The Nonconformist*. However partisan their opponents must have considered this view, Dale and Miall claimed that 'a free Church in a free State' spelled the victory of religion, whether Anglican or Nonconformist. The struggle was arduous and prolonged, but Edward Miall (1809–81) lived to see the abolition of church rates, the opening of the universities of Oxford and Cambridge to Nonconformity, and the Disestablishment of the Irish Church, though not of the English Church.

The concessions were obtained only after prolonged and bitter campaigns. A Bill to introduce the abolition of church rates was decisively defeated in 1836, in which year the same fate befell a proposal to relax the subscriptions for Dissenters who wished to enter the ancient English universities. A minor victory was gained two years later, when it was no longer necessary for Dissenting parents to go to the parish incumbent for the registration of the births of their children, nor for Nonconformist couples to hallow their marriages in an Anglican church. In the same year the Church-Rate Abolition Society was founded, but several Bills drafted to implement its policy proved fruitless. In 1852 Parliament drafted a new series of Burial Laws, which took cognizance of Nonconformist scruples to the extent of allowing a part of every public cemetery to be set aside as 'unconsecrated ground' for Dissenters, and in which they might conduct burials according to the Free Church forms of service. It was not, however, until 1880 that Free Church ministers were authorized to officiate in consecrated ground in cemeteries. Educational privileges were granted even more reluctantly. Oxford allowed Nonconformist students to read for the degree of Bachelor of Arts in 1854, whilst Cambridge granted the same concession in 1856, also allowing Nonconformists to enter for the degree of Master of Arts. In 1871 Oxford, Cambridge, and Durham opened their doors to Dissenters so wide that every privilege of a student was theirs, except that of holding an official position on the staffs of the Colleges.[1] Eleven years later headships and fellowships were also open to Free Churchmen, the sole Anglican prerogative that remained being the election to the chairs of Divinity, still reserved for members of the Establishment. Before this time, of course, Nonconformists had collaborated with benevolent humanists in the foundation of the modern universities, such as University College, London, deliberately established on a non-sectarian basis, and the later universities of Birmingham, Bristol, Liverpool, Manchester, Leeds, and Sheffield.

The most gruelling struggle, however, was in the field of public and elementary education: this battle was waged, almost without an armistice, from 1820 until 1902. It may be thought curious that the ecclesiastical interests should loom so large in what might be regarded as primarily a State responsibility. The answer is that the Churches, Anglican and Non-conformist, were in the van of education many years before the State recognized its responsibility. The public education of the working-classes was first under-taken in the Sunday Schools founded by Robert Raikes, Hannah More, and their Nonconformist imitators. Instruction in reading was given during Sunday after-noons in hundreds of Sunday Schools throughout the country at the beginning of the century. Public day

---

[1] Except that degrees in divinity (D.D. and B.D.) were not opened to them until 1918.

schools owe their origin to a Quaker and an Anglican. The Quaker was Joseph Lancaster (1778–1838) who began teaching poor boys before 1801 and in a few years had a free school for over a thousand boys. His remarkable pioneering methods were set forth in a pamphlet of 1803, entitled *Improvements in Education*. The Anglican educationalist, Andrew Bell (1753–1832), seems to have discovered the monitorial system independently of Lancaster. They both reduced staff and expenditure by setting older pupils to teach the younger, Bell having first tried out his system when superintendent of the Madras Male Orphan Asylum, publishing an account of his successful experiments in 1797. Bell, as a clergyman, naturally insisted upon Anglican divinity lessons being taught to the pupils in the schools that followed his system, the most famous of which was Christ's Hospital. Lancaster, as might be expected, was equally insistent that only 'undenominational' religious instruction should be given in the schools under his aegis. Both groups of schools became popular and both educationalists appealed to the public for monetary support. In 1808 the Royal Lancastrian Society was founded to co-ordinate instruction given in all the schools of Lancaster's pattern, and as the organization grew its name was suitably changed to a more inclusive alternative, 'The British and Foreign School Society'. This move was countered by Bell's supporters who described their organization in 1811 as 'The National Society for promoting the Education of the Poor in the Principles of the Established Church'. By the middle of the century almost every village had its 'British' or its 'National' School, sometimes it had both. The supporters of each type of school did their utmost to obtain the national monopoly.

In 1820 the eighty years' battle began, when Lord Brougham introduced into the Commons a Bill to bring the public elementary education of the country under Anglican control. This he proposed to do by ensuring that schoolmasters must be Anglican communicants, and that they should be appointed in each case by the parish clergyman, assisted by two or three parishioners. Attendance at the parish church was to be compulsory for pupils, though Nonconformist children would be permitted to attend chapel if accompanied by their parents. As for religious instruction, this was simply to take the form of Bible-reading in school. To the immense relief of the harassed Nonconformists the Bill proceeded no further than the first hearing. Henceforth it became clear that a national problem demanded a national not a partisan solution.

In 1833 Roebuck and Grote attempted to persuade Parliament to adopt a national scheme, but this failed. One result, however, was that the Chancellor of the Exchequer, Althorp, suggested that £20,000 should be allocated annually from the Treasury to be divided between the 'British' and 'National' Schools. The disadvantage, as far as the Nonconformists were concerned, was the proviso that the grant should be proportionate to the amount raised by each society from the general public. As the National Society was supported by the upper income-groups, it received much greater Treasury assistance than did the British and Foreign Society.

The next development came in 1840, when an Education Committee of the Privy Council was set up, charged with administering an additional £10,000 in grants and the establishment of a 'Normal College' for the training of teachers. It was stipulated that the

instruction in this College should be on an interdenominational basis, which roused the wrath of the
more vehement Anglicans.

The succeeding rounds of the educational contest
went in favour of the Anglicans, for Peel's Home
Secretary, Sir John Graham, introduced his Factory
Bill in 1844, providing compulsory education for all
children in manufacturing areas. These new schools
were to be financed from three sources in equal propor-
tions: the poor rates, grants, and public subscriptions.
The Bill failed, however, because it insisted that the
clergyman of each parish should have supervising
authority over appointments, instruction, and discipline.

By 1850 the situation had worsened for the Nonconformists, for the two School Societies undertook all the
responsibility for the nation's public education, and the
National Society was increasing in prestige, endow-
ments, and numbers. The unfortunate result was that
many Nonconformists seemed to think that education
should not be in the hands of the Government at all,
because it had penalized their children. The more
moderate Nonconformists, however, held the view that
while the Government should accept responsibility for
providing educational facilities for the nation's children,
it was not its duty to subsidize religious instruction, no
matter what form that might take. Though the Nonconformists did not realize it, the logic of their position
was driving them to exclude instruction in the Christian
faith from the schools of the country. Their opponents
lost no opportunity of reminding them of this.

In 1870 the Government accepted its responsibility
for national education in Foster's Education Act of that
year. Its main provisions were: the erection of schools
in districts where educational facilities were inadequate;

the supervision of such schools to be undertaken by School Boards representative of local interests; and religious instruction to be undenominational, whilst any parents who objected were to be allowed under the 'Cowper-Temple Clause' to withdraw their children from such religious instruction. The Bill was strenuously opposed by Dr. R. W. Dale and Dr. Guinness Rogers in a series of public meetings, with the effect that the revised version of the Bill proved less unsatisfactory than the first draft as far as the Nonconformists were concerned.[1] The more far-seeing Dissenters perceived, however, that if their children were withdrawn from the classes of religious instruction, and taught by their own ministers, this would tend to strengthen the specifically Anglican content of the supposedly undenominational teaching in the schools. Hence the Cowper-Temple Clause, intended as a safeguard of the Free Church interest, was playing into the hands of the Establishment. A disappointed Nonconformity received the last of a long series of slights in 1902 when Balfour's Education Act threw the denominational schools along with the undenominational on the public rates. Here, so it appeared to Free Churchmen, the State was subsidizing denominational interests unashamedly. Once again, since the vast majority of denominational schools belonged to the Established Church, the State had shown itself partisan, despite the fact that the numbers of Nonconformist communicants now equalled the number of Anglican communicants in the country.

Of the public education controversy as a whole, it must be confessed that the victors were the Anglicans,

[1] A. W. W. Dale, *The Life of R. W. Dale of Birmingham*, p. 285 f.

even in the days of a Liberal Government counting heavily on Nonconformist votes. What is more disturbing to record is that by means of this controversy the fissure between 'church' and 'chapel' was widened, and personal relationships between clergy and ministers which promised such felicity in the joint religious and philanthropic enterprises undertaken at the beginning of the century, became increasingly embittered in the second part of the period.

It brought, however, at least one positive advantage to Nonconformity in stimulating the Free Churches to establish their own educational foundations. The Methodists, for example, with Kingswood School, Bath (founded in 1740), as their model established Woodhouse Grove School in 1812, and the Leys School in Cambridge in 1875. The same denomination established Westminster and Southlands Training Colleges, respectively in 1851 and 1872. Nor were they behind-hand in founding theological colleges, establishing Didsbury in Manchester (1842), Richmond in London (1843), Headingley in Leeds (1868), and Handsworth in Birmingham (1881).[1]

The Congregationalists also founded or co-operated in the foundation of several leading schools during the century, notably Mill Hill in London, Caterham in Surrey, and Silcoates in Yorkshire. Many of their Dissenting Academies of the previous century were the nursing mothers of their theological colleges, amongst which were Hackney and New Colleges in London, Western College in Bristol, Lancashire Independent College in Manchester, Yorkshire United Independent College in Bradford, Paton College in Nottingham, and Spring Hill College in Birmingham, which was removed

[1] cf. Maldwyn Edwards, *Methodism and England*.

L

to Oxford and renamed Mansfield College in 1886.[1]
The last-named was the first of the Free Church
theological colleges to be established in either of
the most ancient English universities and owes its
wide-spread fame to the fact that it is exclusively
a post-graduate College, with an ecumenical roll of
alumni, and an academic staff which has included
names of international repute in their respective
fields. Its example was to be followed in 1901 by the
removal of Cheshunt College to Cambridge, whilst the
Methodists established Wesley House in the same
university.

Baptist theological colleges established or refounded
during the nineteenth century include Rawdon College
near Leeds, the Bristol Baptist College, Regent's Park
College in London, and Spurgeon's College in South
London. Following the example of Mansfield and
Cheshunt, Regent's Park College was removed to
Oxford in 1928. The Unitarians had theological
colleges in Manchester and then in Oxford, whilst
the Presbyterians sent their ordinands to be trained
in the Divinity Faculties of the Scottish universities,
until the establishment of Westminster College,
founded in London in 1844 and removed to Cambridge in 1899.

The contributions of the Free Church colleges to
theological education may be summarized as follows:
in systematic theology ordinands were equipped both
to expound and to defend the historic Christian faith;
their exposition of the Scriptures was assisted by
instruction in the Biblical languages, with courses on
literary and historical criticism; comparative religion

---

[1] F. Heiler described Mansfield College Chapel as 'the most
Catholic place in Oxford'.

taught them the distinctive features of the Christian faith and provided elementary missionary training; modern as well as patristic and medieval church history was taught; homiletics and pastoral psychology were the liaison-officers between their academic studies and their vocations as future ministers of the Word of God in the churches. So comprehensive and relevant a course of study was necessarily a lengthy preparation for their calling, and the ideal length of the training was six years, the first three of which were to be spent in acquiring a general education (such as the B.A. degree provides), followed by the three years' post-graduate study of divinity (such as the B.D. degree provides). As a result the ministry of the Free Churches became more and more a teaching ministry; where passionate Christian convictions were blended with a mind made broad and incisive by intellectual exercises and comprehensive studies, this was unparalleled gain; where the prophetic 'Thus saith the Lord' was replaced by the philosophic 'It may be reasonable to suppose' it was irreparable loss. On the whole the gains were greater than the losses, as may be seen in the many distinguished scholar-preachers of the Victorian era, and in the attendance of scholarly and cultured persons in Free Church congregations. Nonconformity was refuting the reproach of philistinism.

A very remarkable feature of Victorian Noncon-formity was its contribution to the amelioration of social conditions created by the 'dark, Satanic mills' of the industrial revolution. On the whole, with the single exception of the Wesleyan ministers in the first half of the century, Nonconformists espoused Liberalism, and even, in some cases, Radicalism. The contribution of Methodism, in particular, to the elevation, educationally and socially, of the 'submerged tenth' is a most significant one.[1]

Methodism appears to have held two attitudes towards the aspirations of the working-classes: the one view conservative, even reactionary, as typified by Dr. Jabez Bunting (1779–1858), for many years a veritable dictator amongst the Wesleyans and a high Tory, and the other view sympathetic to radicalism. Bunting denounced such Wesleyan preachers as favoured the Chartists, and was notorious for the pronouncement 'Wesleyanism is as much opposed to democracy as it is to sin'.[2] It seems that Bunting inherited John Wesley's political rosette,[3] but not his prophetic mantle, for the great evangelist wrote in enthusiastic approbation of Wilberforce's crusade against slavery:

Unless the Divine power had raised you up to be as *Athanasius contra mundum*, I see not how you can go through your glorious enterprise, in opposing that execrable villainy, which is the scandal of religion, of England, and of human nature. . . . Go on, in the name of God and in the power of His might, till even American slavery (the vilest that ever saw the sun) shall vanish away before it.[4]

It may be that Bunting was unnecessarily trembling for the ark of God in the hands of Cobden, but it is certain that he alienated the sympathies of the rank and file of Wesleyanism by his autocratic conservatism. Eventually Methodism rid itself of his hierarchical incubus only by forming new connexions based on a

[1] cf. R. F. Wearmouth, *Methodism and the Working-Class Movements of England* (1937).
[2] Ed. G. M. Young, *Early Victorian England*, II, p. 470.
[3] Disraeli in *Coningsby* describes the Methodists as 'a preserve of the Tory party'.
[4] John Wesley, *Works*, XIII, pp. 127–8.

more democratic form of church government. At the close of the century S. E. Keeble and Hugh Price Hughes had successfully raised the cry of 'Social Christianity' within Wesleyan Methodism. In the interval it was the Primitive Methodists, in the main, who allied themselves with the struggle of the working-classes for better living and working conditions.[1]

According to Halévy, it was the Methodist concern for social justice allied to a reverence for law, which safeguarded England from the political revolutions on the continent of Europe.[2] It may be that Socialism has rarely been anti-clerical in its English manifestations because Nonconformist religion was never 'the opium of the masses'. Nonconformity was at no time the religion of the upper classes, and Methodism most certainly had a large following amongst the working-classes. Its cause was theirs. Halévy writes:

> The majority of the leaders of the great trade union movement that would arise in England within a few years of 1815 will belong to Nonconformist sects. They will often be local preachers. Their spiritual ancestors were the founders of Methodism. In the vast work of social organization, which is one of the dominant characteristics of nineteenth century England, it would be difficult to overestimate the part played by the Wesleyan Revival.[3]

Bunting might play the part of Canute, but the tide of reform was rising. In 1841, for example, 700 Nonconformist ministers assembled under the ensign of the Anti-Corn Law League to fight with Cobden and

[1] cf. Sidney Webb, *The Story of the Durham Miners.*
[2] É. Halévy, *The History of the English People* (Engl. tr.), I, p. 371.
[3] *op. cit.*, I, p. 372.

Bright. Furthermore, three of Shaftesbury's associates in the struggle for better industrial conditions had Methodist associations. Michael Sadler (1780–1835) had preached for Methodist societies whilst still a youth, and he was the chosen parliamentary leader of radical working men, and was appointed Chairman of the Committee for the Factory Report of 1831. Richard Oastler (1789–1861), the son of a local preacher, himself a keen Methodist, was known as 'the factory child's king' for his unremitting labours on behalf of adolescent factory employees. The third of the trio who supported Shaftesbury was a Methodist minister, J. R. Stephens (1805–79), who joined the Chartists in 1838, and was the greatest orator of the group of industrial reformers. It is to Shaftesbury and his three assistants that the English working-classes owed the appearance of the Factory Acts on the Victorian Statute-Book.[1]

In two other aspects Nonconformists also contributed to the social betterment of the working-classes: in the foundation of orphanages and in the crusade for temperance. In both these concerns Wesley was the pioneer, for he had founded an orphan house in Newcastle and a free 'Dispensary for the Sick Poor' in London in 1746, and he inveighed freely against the contemporary over-indulgence in alcoholic liquors. Leading Dissenting orphanages founded during the century were those of George Muller (a Plymouth Brother), Spurgeon (a Baptist minister), T. B. Stephenson (a Methodist) and Dr. Barnardo's Homes (with affinities with both the Baptists and the Brethren).

---

[1] J. E. Rattenbury, *Wesley's Legacy to the World*, pp. 238 ff. Other Methodist social reformers of distinction were Thomas Burt, M.P., the leader of the miners, and Joseph Arch, the founder of the Agricultural Workers' Union.

It was Benjamin Waugh, a Congregational minister, who was co-founder of the London Society for the Prevention of Cruelty to Children, which became the National Society in 1888. The most notable leaders of the Temperance Movement were 'the Seven Men of Preston', most of them lay preachers and Methodists, who took a pledge of total abstinence in 1830. Through their example and influence 'Bands of Hope' for the encouragement of total-abstinence pledges by children soon became a popular feature of Free Church life. Great as the evils of drink were during this period, it is possible that Nonconformity's negative device 'Total Abstinence' lost many adherents who might have rallied to the colours, if they had been emblazoned 'Temperance'.

From the middle of the century Nonconformity was a political force to be reckoned with. In their democratic forms of church government the leaders of the trade union movement had learned the art of responsible government and of speech-making. From the Religious Revival they had learned the common brotherhood of men under the Fatherhood of God. Increasingly Nonconformity became identified with the Liberal Party. It had its own representative, John Bright the Quaker, in the Government itself. As Payne writes: 'Bright, a man of outstanding Christian character, was the first Nonconformist since William Penn to be prominent as a political leader.'[1] The leader of the Midland Liberals was the Unitarian, Joseph Chamberlain, whilst another Unitarian, C. P. Scott, was editor of the most influential Liberal Newspaper, the *Manchester Guardian*. The sounding-boards of the

[1] E. A. Payne, *The Free Church Tradition in the Life of England*, p. 118.

'Nonconformist conscience' during the latter part of the period were the pulpits of Dr. R. W. Dale of Birmingham, and of Hugh Price Hughes in West London. Their allies were the editors of the Free Church newspapers founded during the century. Edward Miall founded and edited *The Nonconformist* in 1841 and sixteen years later *The Christian World* began publication. Hugh Price Hughes started *The Methodist Times* in 1885, and *The British Weekly* appeared a year later, soon to gain renown under the editorship of Sir William Robertson Nicoll. These preachers and editors thundered forth the social implications of the Gospel, refusing to let men sleep in their sins. Dissent was thus closely, perhaps too closely, allied with Liberalism. The reasons for the close liaison are two: the Reform Act of 1832 had enfranchised the ranks from which the Nonconformists were drawn, and politics was moving towards democracy, the very principle which the Free Churches were supposed to enshrine in their form of Church government. It was significant that Palmerston prophesied: 'In the long run English politics will follow the consciences of the Dissenters.' [1] A privileged State Church inevitably stood for the *status quo*, but the Free Churches in fighting for their rights became automatically the champions of the underprivileged from whom they drew their vast membership in the industrial cities. To the prediction of a Tory Prime Minister, cited above, may be added the prophecy of a Whig Prime Minister, Lord John Russell: 'I know the Dissenters. They carried the Reform Bill; they carried the abolition of slavery; they carried Free Trade; and they'll carry the abolition of Church

[1] Cited H. W. Clark, *History of English Nonconformity*, II, p. 402.

Rates.' [1] The vast social and philanthropic enterprises of Victorian England owed their inspiration and support to the combination of the Anglican Evangelicals and the Free Churchmen. England, it seems, escaped a political revolution only because a silent social evolution was taking place, stimulated by the 'Nonconformist conscience'.

The virility of Victorian Free Churchmanship can best be seen in its representative figures, herculean preachers with the voices of a Stentor and the stamina of marathon runners. It is recorded in the life of John Angell James, minister of Carr's Lane Church, Birmingham, that when that divine was preaching the Annual Sermon of the London Missionary Society, he broke off at the end of an hour through sheer exhaustion, and the congregation sang a hymn. Whilst he rested, oranges were thrown into the pulpit to refresh him, and he then 'thundered on for another hour'.[2] During the first quarter of the century the leading preachers among the Congregationalists were: Clayton and Collier in London, John Angell James in Birmingham, William Jay in Bath, and Dr. Bogue in Gosport; among the Baptists the outstanding divines were Robert Hall, the Rylands, father and son, Andrew Fuller, Joseph Kinghorn and John Foster. During the second half of the century the great names were R. W. Dale of Birmingham and Joseph Parker of London's City Temple (Congregationalists); C. H. Spurgeon and Alexander Maclaren, respectively of London and Manchester (Baptists); Hugh Price Hughes of West London (Methodist), and James Martineau of

[1] Cited Payne, *op. cit.*, p. 102.
[2] *Life*, p. 144, cited in A. W. W. Dale, *Life of R. W. Dale of Birmingham*, p. 199.

Liverpool and London (Unitarian). Perhaps John Watson was the best known Presbyterian divine of England during the period, both as minister of Sefton-Road Church, Liverpool, and, under the pseudonym of 'Ian Maclaren', as the writer of charming stories. Three of this number deserve, in their representative capacity, further consideration: R. W. Dale as a preacher of social righteousness and as a theologian; Hugh Price Hughes as the voice of the 'Nonconformist conscience' and co-architect of the National Free Church Council established in 1896; and C. H. Spurgeon as the pre-eminent preacher of the century.

R. W. Dale (1829–95) will always be associated with his civic ministry in Birmingham, where he was one of a long line of distinguished ministers of the Carr's Lane Congregational Church, which has included John Angell James, J. H. Jowett, S. M. Berry, Leyton Richards and Leslie Tizard. He came as assistant to J. A. James and remained as pastor until his death over forty years later. Great as were his influence and reputation in the Midlands, he became a national figure, sitting on the Royal Commission for Education, and receiving the honorary D.D. of Yale and the honorary LL.D. of Glasgow. He attained distinction as a preacher of the civic responsibilities of Christians, as a great Free Church historian and exponent of the doctrine of a 'free church in a free State', as a leading educationalist and the virtual founder of Mansfield College, Oxford, and as a theologian who gained inter-denominational honours, winning even the approbation of Cardinal Newman for his classic volume, *The Atonement*.[1]

He believed that Christian convictions either issued

[1] A. W. W. Dale, *op. cit.*, p. 325.

in political action, or they evaporated in pietistical
sentiment. He once said: 'I feel a grave and solemn
conviction, which deepens year by year, that in a
country like this, where the public business of the State
is the private duty of every citizen, those who decline
to use their political power are guilty of treachery both
to God and to man.' [1] He was associated with Joseph
Chamberlain in the educational and social betterment
of the Midland city. When Chamberlain was returned
to the House as member for Birmingham, a London
daily claimed that 'Mr. R. W. Dale of Birmingham
nominated Mr. Chamberlain, and the will of Mr.
Dale is the will of Birmingham.' To this accusation
Chamberlain replied: '. . . Well, if that be so, there is
not a member of the House of Commons who will have
a better, wiser, or nobler constituency.' [2] He maintained that it was only as men translated their Christian
faith into positive programmes for the benefit of their
underprivileged neighbours that they fulfilled the law
of God, and avoided becoming victims of an 'exquisitely
delicate and valetudinarian spirituality'. He worked on
educational and social service committees, and spoke
on political platforms, to exemplify the civic virtues in
himself.

He was not less renowned as an expositor and
defender of Free Church principles. In a statement
made in his ordination service he stated convictions which were to deepen with the passage of the
years:

I dissent from the Church of England because I
believe that the visible Church of Christ is a congregation of faithful men. . . . I cannot admit that the

[1] A. W. W. Dale, *op. cit.*, p. 250.
[2] *op. cit.*, p. 421.

heterogeneous mass of godly and godless people who equally belong to the National Establishment constitute a Christian Church.[1]

The secret of his Free Churchmanship is surely to be found in the importance for him of the Reformation doctrine of 'the priesthood of all believers.' According to Dale every Christian had to be a priest and all were on the same footing before God, equally with St. Peter charged to feed Christ's lambs. This also explains what some of his contemporaries regarded as his eccentricity in refusing the title of 'Reverend' for himself, for he believed that this was to claim exceptional spiritual authority for the ministry and to institute a double standard of Christian ethics, a higher ministerial and a lower laic level of attainment. He instituted the custom at Carr's Lane of requesting the Church Meeting to appoint a layman once a year to celebrate the Sacrament of Holy Communion, as a reminder of the priesthood of all Christians.[2]

As an educationalist he served both his city and his country well, and his scholarship and catholicity were given full rein in the negotiations for the transfer of Spring Hill College from Birmingham to Oxford, where it was renamed Mansfield College. Writing to Fairbairn, the first Principal, about the statuary in the Chapel of the College, he expressed a preference for '. . . some other group of twelve, e.g. four great theologians of the Catholic Church, including the East and West, e.g. Augustine, Athanasius, Chrysostom and Gregory; then the English Augustine and Wyclif, Luther and Calvin, Cartwright, Robinson, Owen and

---

[1] Dale, *op. cit.*, p. 104.
[2] Though Brewster, although a ruling elder, was not allowed the same privilege on the *Mayflower*.

Howe . . . or, striking out Chrysostom and Gregory, there might be à Kempis and Aquinas'.[1] It is altogether fitting that in the array of nineteenth-century men of God, Dale should find a place with Livingstone in the stained-glass windows of Mansfield Chapel.

Hugh Price Hughes (1847–1902) resembled Dale, as the expositor of the 'Nonconformist conscience' and as a civic reformer. Both preachers were reformers, with a profound sense of the catholicity of the Church. Hughes was evangelical in faith, and radical in politics, and these convictions were seen both in *The Methodist Times*, the organ of the Methodist Forward Movement, which he edited from 1885, and in his book, *Social Christianity*, issued in 1890.

As the leader of the Methodist Forward Movement, he planned the strategy of advance into the slums of the great cities. Its first great triumphs were the founding of Missions in East London (1885), Manchester (1885), Central London (1886), West London (1887), South London (1889), South West London (1899), Poplar and Bow (1900), and Deptford (1903). Hughes was appointed superintendent of the West London Mission at its foundation, when there was some scepticism about the future of a mission in the midst of a well-to-do area. His challenging and fearless preaching, however, proved the magnet for all sorts and conditions of men. Moreover, he developed the system of Methodist sisterhoods, virtually acting as assistant ministers, but without the 'objectionable vows' (his own phrase) of perpetual celibacy. His daughter writes about his convictions at this time: 'Bit by bit, Christ was to dawn on this disciple as the greatest social reformer the world had yet known—in sympathy, not only with the classes

[1] *op. cit.*, p. 503.

who shouted for order, but with the masses who rebelled against that order because their interests had not been considered in it.'[1] Hughes was so profoundly concerned for the spiritual and social redemption of men that he joined, in his own words, 'the noble army of agitators'. The stiff bones of Dr. Jabez Bunting must have stirred uneasily in his grave; but Hughes knew that the Methodist disruption of 1849 was entirely due to the fathers of the Conference stifling Liberal sympathies within the fold, and costing Wesleyan Methodism tens of thousands of members and adherents. Hughes, therefore, made it his aim to reconquer the lost provinces of Methodism amongst the working-classes.

He will, however, go down to history as the midwife at the birth of the 'Nonconformist conscience'. Hughes was the supporter of Irish Home Rule until the leader, Parnell, alienated his sympathies as co-respondent in a divorce suit, which was undefended by Parnell. The General Election was at hand and Parnell's action placed the Liberals in a dilemma: either to retain his vigorous leadership and offend the moral sense of the Nonconformist supporters of Liberalism, or to retain the approbation of Nonconformity and to lose Parnell. On the Sunday following the court case, Hughes was announced to speak on the controversial issue in the St. James's Hall. The atmosphere was tense, for there were journalists, politicians, and an Irish contingent there, in addition to the usual congregation. His concluding peroration, reported in all the newspapers of the kingdom, is believed to have influenced Gladstone to ask for Parnell's resignation. It read:

[1] D. P. Hughes, *The Life of Hugh Price Hughes by his Daughter*, p. 81.

We love Ireland. We passionately desire her well-being; but our first obedience and our highest devotion must be to God. We have sacrificed much for Ireland. She is entitled to many sacrifices at our hands; but there is one thing we will never sacrifice, and that is our religion. We stand immovably on this eternal rock; what is morally wrong can never be politically right.[1]

One of Parnell's supporters wrote in the correspondence columns of the London *Times* that Hughes was motivated not by Christianity, but by 'the Nonconformist conscience'. Hughes accepted the praise as a proud trophy of victory, and used it as a battle-cry in his further campaigns.

The 'social Gospel' and catholicity were outstanding features of a memorable series of biographical addresses he gave in the St. James's Hall to crowded congregations. His verbal portraits included Father Damien, Catherine Booth, St. Francis of Assisi, General Gordon, John Wesley, Cardinal Newman, John Bright, Mazzini, Bruno, Tennyson, and Browning.

The Free Churches of England owe him a great debt, for it was due to the advocacy and statesmanship of Hughes, and of Dr. Charles Berry of Wolverhampton, that the National Free Church Council was established in 1896. Protestantism, as he saw it, was an undisciplined mob; the separated Free Churches must confederate to have a sense of being part of the one Holy Catholic Church. Further, he believed that each denomination required the complementary emphases of the other denominations to give it a full-orbed life. He was uncompromising in his approbation of Free Churchmanship, declaring: 'The present method

[1] *op. cit.*, pp. 351 ff. Cf. H. F. Lovell Cocks, *The Nonconformist Conscience.*

of union between the Church and the State tends to make the Church worldly, without making the world Christian.'[1] He entirely subscribed to Cavour's formula: 'A free church in a free State'. Taking a leaf out of the Anglican book, he proposed that a Free Church Congress should be held in 1892, and from this the Free Church Council was to grow. In 1896 he was elected the first President of the National Council of Evangelical Free Churches. He took the major responsibility in drafting the clauses of its constitution, the objects of which are described as follows:

(a) To facilitate fraternal intercourse and cooperation among the Evangelical Free Churches. (b) To assist in the organisation of local councils. (c) To encourage devotional fellowship and mutual counsel concerning the spiritual life and religious activities of the Churches. (d) To advocate the New Testament doctrine of the Church, and to defend the rights of the associated Churches. (e) To promote the application of the law of Christ to every relation of human life.[2]

It was not his least distinction that he was an Ecumenical thinker who was also a High Churchman.

Charles Haddon Spurgeon (1834–92) was the most effective and popular preacher of the nineteenth century, inviting comparison for the size of his congregations with Wesley or Whitefield. As a young man, largely self-taught, he came on probation as the minister of New Park Street Baptist Church in Southwark. Here a congregation of about 200 sat disconsolately in a building accommodating six times that number. Within a year Spurgeon had filled the building, and two years later even the enlarged building proved inadequate. Whilst the renovations were being made, he showed his

[1] Hughes, *op. cit.*, p. 482.   [2] *op. cit.*, p. 448.

initiative by renting the Surrey Gardens Music Hall, and there over 10,000 souls gathered to hear him preach. Here, since his congregation consisted of many who read newspapers until the service commenced, and of ladies and gentlemen who drove up in their carriages but would never have entered a Dissenting conventicle, he proved that religion could be brought to the people, if they would not come to Church. He was paid the compliment of frequent imitation, and had blazed the trail for the Salvation Army and for evangelical meetings in theatres and in the open air. In 1861 the Metropolitan Tabernacle was built at a cost of £31,000 to accommodate his regular congregation of 6,000 people. When the renovation of the Tabernacle was proceeding, he preached for three months to crowds of over 20,000 in the Agricultural Hall, Islington. On 7 October 1857 he preached on a National Fast Day in the Crystal Palace to a gathering of 23,654 persons.

He was not only a powerful and magnetic preacher, but also a great pastor. His congregation was not loosely attached to the preacher, but integrated in the Body of Christ. During the thirty-eight years of his London ministry, he gathered, built, and held together a congregation of 6,000 souls. During this time he added 14,692 members to the Church, an annual average of 387.[1]

The preacher and pastor was also an efficient administrator. He founded in 1856 the Pastors' College (known to-day as Spurgeon's College), which had trained 1,045 Baptist ministers by 1903,[2] and in 1867 an undenominational orphanage in Stockwell, which

[1] C. Ray, *The Life of Charles Haddon Spurgeon* (1903), pp. 495–6.
[2] *op. cit.*, p. 342.

M

had acted as Christian foster-parent to 2,423 children
by the turn of the century. He also founded a Col-
portage Association for the dissemination of religious
tracts and Bibles, and edited the evangelical periodical,
The Sword and Trowel.

His influence on his own denomination was considerable, but his friendships were interdenominational.
He initiated the 'Downgrade Controversy' in his periodical, attacking the Modernism that held the Fall to be a
fable, the Resurrection a hallucination, and that sub-
stituted for the conditional future life of the Gospels an
amoral universalism which they were pleased to call
'the larger hope'. He left the Baptist Union because
that body would not impose a confession of faith upon
its ministers, but his challenge had the effect of arousing
amongst all evangelical ministers a vigilant fidelity to
the faith once delivered to the saints, and of persuading
many of them that a creed or a confession was a valuable
safeguard against heresy, and a pointer to the apostolic
faith. His influence beyond the limits of his own
denomination is proved by the breadth of his friendships and acquaintances, among whom he numbered
Archbishop Benson, W. E. Gladstone, Bishops Thorold
and Welldon, Dean Stanley, and D. L. Moody the
evangelist.

Many factors may be adduced to account for his outstanding success as a preacher. He stated that he took
George Whitefield as his model. He had undoubted
oratorical ability, both in the impassioned directness of
his appeals and in his vivid illustrations. He was un-
afraid of humour in the pulpit, and made a virtue of
being understood by the humblest of men. Indeed, he
criticized much of the current preaching for its un-
intelligibility, declaring: 'Christ said, "Feed my sheep,

feed my lambs." Some preachers, however, put the food so high, that neither lambs nor sheep can reach it. They seem to have read the text, "Feed my giraffes".' [1] He took to heart the advice of Goethe to a preacher, 'Don't give us your doubts; give us your certainties, for we have doubts enough of our own.' In an age when biology and theology were in conflict, he did not reason out his doctrines; he announced them, illustrated them and applied them. His vocabulary avoided Latinity, keeping to the terse and thrusting Anglo-Saxon words. But the great preacher is a gift of God; we may be instructed by his craftsmanship but we cannot fathom his Divine call. If we seek for parallels, we may say that he was as vigorous and homely as Latimer preaching before the king, as humorous as South berating Rochester the libertine, and as declamatory as White-field moving Hume or Chesterfield to admiration.

The most significant and epoch-making feature of the period has yet to be chronicled: that is the modern missionary movement which arose within English Non-conformity, and received its sacrificial support in men and money. The Society for the Propagation of the Gospel in Foreign Parts, an Anglican enterprise, was founded in 1701, but it was intended primarily to minister to the spiritual needs of English settlers in the North American Colonies. Indeed, it may be claimed, with some justice, that the parent of this Society was the ordinance passed by the Independents of the Commonwealth on 27 July 1648, constituting a corporation under the title, 'The President and Society for the Propagation of the Gospel in New England'. Other influences were the Evangelical Revival, whose leader

[1] Ray, *op. cit.*, p. 234.

had declared that 'the world is my parish', and the philanthropic enterprises of a Wilberforce and a Raikes, in which the principles of the revolutionary Levellers were commingled with the Christian doctrine of man.

Whatever the remote causes, the proximate cause and origin of the modern missionary movement was the conviction of a Baptist shoemaker-teacher-minister that Protestants had been unaccountably blind in face of their responsibilities for world evangelism. William Carey (1761–1834) was prepared for his calling as a missionary statesman by conversion as a youth, by his growing interest in geography and foreign languages, stimulated by reading the accounts of the voyages of Captain Cook, and by the heroic examples of St. Paul and John Eliot and David Brainerd, who laboured amongst the American Indians. He prepared *An Enquiry into the Obligations of Christians to use Means for the Conversion of the Heathens.* His thesis was that the dominical command to 'preach the gospel to every creature' was as binding on the Christians of the eighteenth century as on the Apostles. He gave in outline a history of successive attempts made by Christians to fulfil the obligation, and provided a survey of the populations and religions professed by the countries of the world. Finally, he offered practical proposals for making good the deficiency.

He succeeded in persuading his fellow ministers in the Midlands of the feasibility and desirability of world-evangelism in a sermon preached in Nottingham in 1792, which contained the memorable phrases: 'Expect great things from God. Attempt great things for God.' At a meeting called in Kettering on 2 October 1792 'The Particular Baptist Society for Propagating the Gospel amongst the Heathen' was established. This became known later as 'The Baptist Missionary Society'. Carey was one of the original contingent of missionaries sent out by the Society to India. His enthusiasm and example proved contagious.[1]

The London Missionary Society was founded as an imitation of the Baptist Missionary Society, and it was a letter dispatched by Carey from India to Dr. Ryland which led to its foundation. Although it drew its main support from the Congregational churches, it was established upon an ecumenical foundation, for the founding fathers included John Love and James Steven (Presbyterian divines) and Dr. Haweis, the Anglican chaplain to the Countess of Huntingdon, as well as such Congregational ministers as Mr. Burder of Coventry and Dr. Bogue of Gosport. Its astonishingly advanced 'fundamental principle' declares:

our design is not to send Presbyterianism, Independency, Episcopacy, or any other form of Church Order and Government (about which there may be differences of opinion among serious Persons), but the Glorious Gospel of the blessed God to the Heathen; and that it shall be left (as it ever ought to be left) to the minds of the Persons whom God may call into the fellowship of His Son from among them to assume for themselves such form of Church Government, as to them shall appear most agreeable to the Word of God.[2]

Many objections had to be met before the new Society was launched, some still current, but many curious.[3]

[1] For the entire subject of modern missionary origins in England see K. S. Latourette, *A History of the Expansion of Christianity* (London, 1947), IV, pp. 64–74.
[2] R. Lovett, *The History of the London Missionary Society* (1899), I, pp. 49–50.
[3] *op. cit.*, I, pp. 34–5.

Dr. Bogue was asked to establish the first missionary seminary in 1800, where, apart from theology and the 'mechanick arts', the intending missionaries are to be taught 'how they may be patient and submissive under disappointments, persevering under long discouragements, ready to meet sufferings or even death, if such should be the divine appointment'.[1] He trained such men as Loveless of Madras, Robert Morrison of China, Carl Pacalt of South Africa, David Jones and David Griffiths of Madagascar.

Soon other interdenominational organizations were founded which assisted the missionary societies, such as the Religious Tract Society (1799), from which emerged the British and Foreign Bible Society (1804), whilst the Sunday School Union was established a year earlier. The great Methodist missionary, Dr. Coke, had been propagating the faith in America and the West Indies in the seventeen-eighties, and from 1790 onwards the Wesleyan Conference took steps to support him. In 1817 the Methodist Missionary Society became the official organ of the Conference. In Scotland the Scottish and the Glasgow Missionary Societies were founded in 1796; whilst the General Assembly of the Church of Scotland appointed a Foreign Missions Committee in 1824, and sent Alexander Duff to India in 1831. The Free Churches were now advancing on a world front as part of the Church militant, and by the end of the century the names of their missionaries were household words. Moffatt, Livingstone, and William Shaw, in Africa; Morrison, Legge, Hill, Griffith John, Hudson Taylor, Gilmour, and Timothy Richard in China; Paton, John Williams, and Chalmers in the South Seas; and Carey, Loveless, and a host of others

1 Lovett, *op. cit.*, I, p. 71.

in India, were symbols of the new confidence of Non-conformity and of its sacrificial love for Christ.

The most distinguished missionary historian writes: 'In geographic extent, in movements issuing from it, and in its effect upon the race, in the nineteenth century Christianity had a far larger place in human history than at any previous time.'[1] In this magnificent enterprise the Free Churches had played the leading part, with the result that in Africa, Asia and Australasia there came into being Christian communities both free and non-episcopal, which fully justified William Carey's great expectations of God. In this extension of the faith, the non-episcopal Churches of America took an equal share with the Free Church Societies of England.

'The great century' of Christian missions is also the great century of the growth of Nonconformity, whether the *criteria* used are statistics, the growth of new organ-izations, or influence on the national life. At the begin-ning of the century there were 270 Presbyterian, 708 Baptist, and 1,024 Congregational congregations, a total of 2,002.[2] If the average congregation numbered about 200 (and the figure is, if anything, too high) that would give a membership of about 400,000. To this may be added the 72,000 members and almost 500,000 adherents of Methodism at Wesley's death in 1791,[3] making a total of a million Nonconformists amongst the four major denominations within Dissent. By 1910, the

[1] K. S. Latourette, *op. cit.*, v, p. 1. Cf. also Latourette, IV, pp. 64 ff. for a study of the factors accounting for British leadership in missions.
[2] H. W. Clark, *History of English Nonconformity* (1911), II, p. 315.
[3] Townshend Workman and Eayrs, *A New History of Methodism* (1909), I, p. 369.

figures had been more than doubled, despite the foundation of new sects and the struggle between modern science and traditional religion. Statistics of that date indicated that the Free Churches had 2,125,275 communicants, while the Anglican communicants numbered 2,231,735. The number of adherents was not given, but the figures for seating accommodation leave little doubt that the Free Churches counted many more adherents than the Establishment. The Free Churches had sittings for 8,788,285 and the Anglicans for 7,236,423.[1]

The resurgence of Nonconformity in the latter half of the nineteenth century owes much to a remarkable revival, described by its historian as 'The Second Evangelical Awakening in Britain'.[2] It is computed that this movement, beginning in Ulster in 1859 and continuing through Scotland, England, and Wales, added a million members to the Evangelical Churches, amongst them such leaders as Tom Barnardo, James Chalmers, Hugh Price Hughes, Evan Hopkins (founder of the Keswick Convention), Alexander Whyte, Timothy Richard, and Sir Robert Anderson (Chief of Scotland Yard). Others impressed by the Revival were Bishops Handley Moule and Francis James Chavasse. From this spiritual renascence arose such influential associations as the Salvation Army, the China Inland Mission (and several interdenominational imitators), and the Children's Special Service Mission. The collaboration of evangelicals of many denominations may well have fostered the beginnings of Ecumenism in the nineteenth century.

The creative movements within the Free Churches

---

[1] Cited W. B. Selbie, *Nonconformity*, pp. 233–4.
[2] J. E. Orr, *op. cit.* (1949).

which led to the foundation of new organizations were manifold. New religious associations founded during the nineteenth century were the Church of the Disciples,[1] the Plymouth Brethren, and the Catholic Apostolic Church, each in its different way an attempt to return to Primitive Christianity. Two other international religious organizations formed during this period were the Young Men's Christian Association (1844), and the Salvation Army (1877), which developed from 'The Christian Revival Association' founded in 1865 by William and Catherine Booth. The pioneers of most of these religious bodies were Free Churchmen: Campbell was a Presbyterian minister before he founded the Disciples, William Booth was a Methodist minister, and Edward Irving was a Presbyterian minister until he founded the Catholic Apostolic Church. Another feature of the century was the proliferation of sects from within Wesleyan Methodism, for the Methodist New Connexion was formed in 1797 and the next quarter-century saw the foundation of Independent Methodists, Bible Christians and Protestant Methodists.

Despite the comfort, commercial prosperity, and imperial expansion of Victorian England, in which the Free Churches shared, Christian orthodoxy was subjected to a series of severe tests, from which none of the English Churches emerged unscathed. Although the Oxford Movement had strengthened the theology and churchmanship and revitalized the worship of the Church of England, and although the Second Evangelical Revival had added almost a million converts to the evangelical Churches in England, neither the Anglican

[1] A. C. Watters, *History of the British Churches of Christ* (1948).

nor the Free Churches were able to repulse the attacks on the orthodox faith. These onsets came from the quarter of the developing natural and social sciences or from the so-called 'higher criticism' of the Biblical documents.

The origins of the unhappy controversy between an infallible scientific world-view and an infallible Biblical world-view could have been found in the Deistic battles of the previous century, but those were mere skirmishes as compared with the open warfare between scientists and theologians in the middle and late decades of the nineteenth century. The first attack, a covert one, came in the shape of Lyell's *Principles of Geology* (1830); the author's thesis was outlined in the sub-title—'being an attempt to explain the former changes of the earth's surface by reference to causes now in operation'. It was clear that the distinguished geologist did not find it necessary to postulate a divine intervention for the creation of the world. The world was, by implication, not the product of a six days' divine activity, but the result of an evolution through millions of years. Hence the orthodox inferred that Lyell was taking very considerable liberties with the Mosaic time-table, to say nothing of Archbishop Ussher's chronology. Furthermore, the author had raised indirectly the problem of the origin of species. The second attack on the citadel of Biblical faith was direct: it was the anonymous publication entitled *The Vestiges of Creation* (1844). The twelfth edition of this work, published forty years later, revealed that the author was Robert Chambers of *Encyclopaedia* fame. The writer began by expounding Laplace's nebular hypothesis as an account of the origin of the solar system, and proceeded to explain the origin of species by evolution. He, too, could have re-echoed

Laplace's retort to Napoleon, on being asked where God came into the scientist's picture, 'Sire, I have no need of that hypothesis.'

The most significant challenge to the old faith was the work of Lyell's pupil, Charles Darwin, in his celebrated *Origin of Species* (1859). This advanced an ingenious theory of the method of evolution, urging that in the struggle for life only the fittest survive. Fitness was understood as ability to adapt to the changing environment, whether by means of superior strength, speed, protective devices, or similar factors.

Thus, the Biblical cosmogony with its account of divine creation was being attacked by the sciences of astronomy, geology, and biology. As a result the hypothesis of God was either made so remote in distance or time as to be almost inconceivable, or it was altogether ignored. These circumstances occasioned a long and largely discreditable warfare between dogmatic materialists and dogmatic bibliolaters.

The concept of evolution was later applied to the fields of sociology, psychology, and ethics by Herbert Spencer in his voluminous *Synthetic Philosophy*, the programme for which appeared in 1862. Despite the disclaimers of Darwin and his 'bulldog' T. H. Huxley, he proceeded to equate the survival of the fittest with the survival of the best. In so doing he placed a heavy premium on the doctrine of inevitable progress, which made theism ethically unnecessary on his premises. Thus, as the natural sciences had repudiated the Christian cosmogony, so the newer social sciences repudiated the Christian doctrines of original sin and redemption, believing that education and social reforms would eliminate the anti-social characteristics of man.

The Christian Churches were, however, most deeply wounded in the house of their friends; that is, by the new school of Biblical criticism which originated in Germany and is associated with the Tübingen critics. Their founder F. C. Baur (1792–1860) put forward most iconoclastic conclusions as to the authority and date of the New Testament documents, with the consequence that radical and rationalist biographies of Jesus of Nazareth were now issued. George Eliot produced her English translation of Strauss's *Leben Jesu* in 1847. Here the Lord of the Church was reduced to the status of a Galilean teacher of morals, who was murdered as the result of an unfortunate collision with the ecclesiastical authorities of the day. Another famous biography, was that of Renan (the *Vie de Jésus* of 1863), which also divested the Eternal Son of God of all the attributes of divinity and all the mystery and the miracles of His Incarnation. In the end, the attacks on the Scriptures and the faith to which they are a testimony produced a more satisfactory Christian apologetics and a deeper understanding of the uniqueness of the Bible and of the historicity of the Founder of the faith. But while the struggle continued, it turned many away from the Churches and forced others to become obscurantist and anti-intellectual in taking up the cudgels for Christianity.

Amongst the English Churches of the Genevan tradition, the Baptists and the Congregationalists suffered most severely from radical Biblical criticism, because the foundation of their church life was exclusively Biblical. The Methodists, with an experiential theology, did not, it may be surmised, suffer to the same extent. The Baptists were seriously divided by the 'Downgrade Controversy', the Liberals who accepted some of the results of the newer Biblical criticism being labelled 'downgrade' by their doughty opponent, the literalist, C. H. Spurgeon.

Victorian literature owes not a little of its pathos to the wistfulness of 'agnostics' (a term invented by T. H. Huxley in 1869 to distinguish doubters from deniers) who figure either as authors or characters in its poems and novels. Matthew Arnold, for example, tried to content himself with 'a Power not ourselves making for righteousness' as a substitute for 'the God and Father of our Lord Jesus Christ', and with 'morality touched with emotion' as a substitute for 'being conformed to the image of His Son'. Clough's poems, Huxley's essays, the novels of Mark Rutherford and Mrs. Humphry Ward, and the family portrait in Gosse's *Father and Son*, describe in different ways the struggle for or the loss of faith. Even the confident Browning and the Laureate Tennyson seem occasionally to be whistling in the dark, as in *Bishop Blougram's Apology* or *In Memoriam*. If a nation's poets and novelists are the sensitive barometers of an age, then the indications were that life in the spirit would continue to be overcast and stormy.

At the close of the century, despite the prevalent hesitancy which hung like a shadow over all religious Communions, the Free Churches were running level, statistically, with the Church of England, but they had outdistanced her in the race for world membership. In 1910 the international figures for Free Church membership were 21,862,092, whilst the corresponding figures for Pan-Anglicanism were 4,022,493.[1] The differences are due, in large measure, to the missionary advances of the Free Churches overseas, and to the great resources

[1] W. B. Selbie, *op. cit.*, p. 234.

of the non-episcopal Communions in the United States of America, themselves the outreaches of seventeenth-century Puritanism and eighteenth-century Methodism in England.

CHAPTER VIII

THE TWENTIETH CENTURY

THE hesitancy which characterized the later decades
of the religious life of the nineteenth century became
acute anxiety in the first decades of the twentieth
century. The Victorian aftermath had set in. It seemed
as if Free Church ministers had either to compromise
with the evolutionary spirit of the age, or to ignore it
altogether. Those who chose the latter path ran the
risk of irrelevancy, whilst those who sought to inte-
grate theology with the results of modern science
were dubbed 'modernists'. Outstanding amongst the
preachers whose chief concern was to be up-to-date
was the Rev. R. J. Campbell, the silver-tongued
minister of the City Temple. His social compassion and
immanental theology attracted many to his services.
He claimed to preach the 'New Theology', which was
a Socialist version of the historic Christian faith, with
Christ the Philanthropist in place of Christ the Saviour.
Its novelty consisted in the rejection of the doctrine of
original sin (the correlate of which is the universal need
of redemption) and in the emphasis on Jesus as social
reformer. As an example of the 'social gospel' it would
be difficult to improve on the following citation from a
City Temple declaration: 'Go with Keir Hardie to the
House of Commons, and listen to his preaching for
justice to his order, and you see the Atonement.'[1] In
this optimistic and evolutionary view of human nature,
Dr. Campbell was merely the sounding-board of the

[1] R. J. Campbell, *The New Theology* (1907), p. 173.

scientists. Only four years before, Sir Oliver Lodge had written: 'The Higher Man of today is not worrying about his sins at all. As for Original Sin or Birth Sin, or other notion of that kind, that sits lightly on him. As a matter of fact it is non-existent, and no one but a monk could have invented it.'[1] Many Free Church ministers found themselves imitating the Anglican hero of Mrs. Humphry Ward's novel, *Robert Elsmere*, in trying to hunt with the evolutionary hounds (scientific or socialist) and run with the Christian hare. Their attempted solution was to work for the social and educational amelioration of the conditions of the under-privileged, rather than for the personal and social redemption of society. Sociology supplanted soteri-ology, but at least the 'social gospellers' and the 'new theologians' could not be accused of fostering an individual and other-worldly pietism. Moreover, if men in general would not acknowledge personal culpability, they readily confessed to communal sins of omission. None the less, of the three great Christian virtues only charity remained, for faith was sickening and hope was moribund.

Such a decay in faith and disbelief in the future life was to be expected when scientists, politicians, and even some theologians, accepted the dogma of inevitable pro-gress. Man stood upon the escalator of ascent, his philosopher Coué, not the Christ, and his ears were open to congratulation and deaf to condemnation. But the gradual and inevitable ascent was rudely halted by the onset of the First World War of 1914, fought between 'progressive' nations, with newly-invented techniques of barbarism. The survivors of that grim

[1] *Hibbert Journal* (1904). Cited R. Lloyd, *The Church of England in the Twentieth Century*, I (1946), p. 39.

encounter with death in the no-man's-land of shrap-
nel, barbed-wire, and mud, became in T. S. Eliot's
phraseology the 'Hollow Men' haunting the 'Waste
Land'. In brief, the day-dream of a Spencerian Utopia
gave way to the Spenglerian nightmare.

The Liberal theology and the Social Gospel were not
entirely discredited, though the dogma of inevitable
progress was at a discount in the post-war disenchant-
ment. For some who returned from the valley of the
shadow, sin was become not so much a recovered word
in their ecclesiastical vocabulary, as an existential fact
of their experience. For others Stoicism, Epicurean-
ism, or aestheticism was preferable to the sentimental
and impracticable demands (as they conceived them) of
the Christian Gospel.

Gradually in the inter-war years, there emerged a
new emphasis in the theology of the Anglican clergy
and the Free Church ministry, though it was expressed
largely by the leaders of Christian thought. This was
the combination of a right-wing orthodoxy in doctrine,
with a left-wing approach to social problems. This was
due to many factors, chief among them a dissatisfaction
with Liberalism in theology and politics; a recognition
of the depth of egotism in man for which the only
remedy was the grace of God in Jesus Christ, transmitted through the Divine-human Community, the
Church; the warnings of the insufficiency of humanism
that came from the Nazi and Fascist tyrannies on the
Continent; a sympathy with the economic egalitarianism of the U.S.S.R. as it set about its herculean Five-
Year Plan; and, most of all, a return on the part of most
Christian Communions to the great historic theologians
and the Bible. Assisted by the expositions and intro-
ductions of Étienne Gilson and Jacques Maritain, many

N

theologians of the Establishment returned to the *Summa Theologiae* of St. Thomas Aquinas, and rediscovered there his comprehensive blending of reason and revelation, of Aristotelian philosophy and Christian doctrine. Free Church teachers found a new relevance in Calvin, as re-interpreted by Karl Barth and Emil Brunner. Sir Edwyn Hoskyns and Professor C. H. Dodd in Cambridge taught a new generation of theological students to appreciate 'realized eschatology', and to read their Bibles as the marching orders of a militant Church, commanded by the crucified and risen Christ. But whether theologians were Neo-Thomist, Neo-Calvinist, or Neo-Biblicist, they agreed in Neo-Orthodoxy.

Theological pilgrimages in the third decade of the century took Free Church ministers occasionally to Canterbury, and sometimes even to Rome.[1] Many, however, remained within the Communions of their allegiance, but took a decided 'right-turn' in doctrine. Like G. K. Chesterton they might have agreed that the Gospel was 'the good news of original sin', or, at least, the good news of how to overcome original sin. As a result more Free Church pulpits became the sounding-boards of divine revelation, in lieu of human revaluations.

At the same time, the Churches were moving to the left sociologically. In this they were helped by the outstanding influence of Dr. William Temple (successively Bishop of Manchester, Archbishop of York, and Archbishop of Canterbury), who found in the central Christian doctrine of the Incarnation the impetus to

---

[1] For such theological Baedekers see W. E. Orchard, *From Faith to Faith* (1933), D. R. Davies, *On to Orthodoxy* (1939), and C. S. Lewis (a brilliant Anglican lay apologist), *Pilgrim's Regress*.

social service, and was for many years the President of the Workers' Educational Association.[1] A similar conviction was found in the writings of Dr. Reinhold Niebuhr, though he drew his inspiration from the well of St. Paul, whereas the future Archbishop drank most deeply of the living water in St. John's Gospel. The cry for social reconstruction came most insistently from the ministers of settlements established in the East End of London or in the slum districts of the great industrial cities.

The first Free Church social crusaders in the present century were Scott Lidgett, John Clifford, and Silvester Horne.[2] The latter had expressed the demand for social justice in the characteristic epigram, 'The ballot-box is the sacrament of human brotherhood.' To the objection, 'No politics in the pulpit', the reformers had retorted, 'No Christianity which is not social'. It is significant that two of this trio lived to become the leaders of the Churches which had regarded them in pre-war years with middle-class anxiety. Dr. Scott Lidgett, who had served as a St. Pancras vestryman with George Bernard Shaw, became the President of the Methodist Conference, and, like Dr. John Clifford, received the award of a Companion of Honour. The social leaven was manifestly leavening the lump.

This growing social concern was seen in the increase of institutional churches and settlements, in the appointment of Social Service Secretaries to the headquarters staffs of the Free Churches, and in the convention of the interdenominational Conference on

[1] cf. F. A. Iremonger, *William Temple*, and M. B. Reckitt, *From Maurice to Temple*.
[2] cf. Sir James Marchant, *Dr. John Clifford C.H.* (1924), and W. B. Selbie, *C. Silvester Horne* (1920).

Politics, Economics, and Citizenship (C.O.P.E.C.) in Birmingham in 1924.

The Churches were not only diagnosing and alleviating the maladies of society, but they were discovering their own unique nature in two important movements, the one liturgical, the other ecumenical. The first represents a recovery in the Free Churches of the importance of divine worship, as distinct from preaching; the second was a concern for closer co-operation, and ultimately for organic reunion, amongst the non-Roman-Catholic Communions.

The pioneers in the reform of Free Church worship owed much both to the Oxford Movement within the Establishment and to the service-books and liturgists of the Church of Scotland. Such Scottish service-books as *Euchologion* (first issued in 1867) and such liturgists as Leishman, Sprott, and Wotherspoon, showed that the Reformed tradition was not to be equated glibly with a rejection of 'stinted forms' of prayer, but was a liturgy according to the Word of God, with its own Biblical architectonic, independent of the predilections of the presiding minister. Their contention was proved by the Church Service Society's reprints of the historic Reformed liturgies, and by the monographs of W. D. Maxwell and Wm. McMillan. The rediscovery of Liturgy was followed at first by indiscriminate 'anthologizing', that is, an arbitrary selection of prayers from incompatible sources. Flowers of devotion were transplanted from Eastern or Italian gardens, ancient or modern, and the result was often a bizarre and incongruous show of blooms, where enthusiasm was a substitute for historical understanding.

Amongst individual ministers of the Free Churches, John Hunter, a Glasgow Congregationalist, led the way with his *Devotional Services for Public Worship* (last revised in 1901), which was as remarkable for its social emphasis as for re-introducing responses to churches of the Puritan tradition. Less well-known, because privately printed, was *The Rodborough Bede Book*, compiled by the Rev. C. E. Watson for the benefit of a rural Congregational community in Gloucestershire, and distinguished for its agricultural imagery, its Anglo-Saxon vocabulary, and its fruits from researches into the worship of the Early Church. The most outstanding liturgy produced by a single minister was Dr. W. E. Orchard's *Divine Service* (1919), for which the author had invaded the kingdom of ancient and modern liturgies like a monarch, and to which he added some exquisitely chaste collects of his own devising. His work is distinguished for its comprehensiveness, which leaves room, in his own words, 'for freely uttered and for silent prayer, not only as existing alongside liturgical forms, but as their very crown and consummation'.[1] Dr. F. B. Meyer and the Rev. F. C. Spurr attempted, if not perhaps with equal success, to provide suitable liturgical alternatives for the Baptist Churches.

More significant than the work of these pioneers in its cumulative effect upon Free Church worship, was the compilation of directories and service-books officially issued by the respective denominations. The English Presbyterians led the liturgical movement with the *Directory of Public Worship* (1898, revised and re-issued in 1921). The Congregationalists published *A Book of Congregational Worship* (1921), a *Manual for Ministers* (1936), and an interesting but unofficial directory, *A Book of Public Worship compiled for the use of Congregationalists* (1948). The Methodists took the

[1] Preface to *Divine Service*.

opportunity of issuing *Divine Worship* only four years after the reunion of three Communions of divergent traditions in worship, and this was published by the authority of the Methodist Conference (1936). The dissemination of the principles and the privileges of worship has been maintained in the Methodist Sacramental Fellowship, its twofold aim being: 'a re-affirmation of Methodism's oneness with the Universal Church, and a strengthened emphasis on sacramental worship'. In these ways, Communions hitherto notable for the passion and prophetic relevance of their preaching, have found the dignity and objectivity of worship. If Newman was able in 1848 to distinguish between Protestant worship as an *invocation* of the Eternal, and Catholic worship as an *evocation* of the Eternal,[1] the point of the contrast would have been lost a century later, for the worship of the Free Churches emphasized the divine initiative in the Sacraments, in the proclamation of the Word, in the round of the Christian Year, and even in its architectural symbolism. There may be some church interiors which proclaim, 'I believe in Geometry', not 'I believe in God'; there may still be some congregations which prefer the sugary subjectivity of a vesper to the sublime objectivity of the Blessing; there may still be those who prefer crouching to kneeling as an attitude of prayer, and chrysanthemums to a cross on the Lord's Table. On the whole, however, there has been a decided improvement in the ordering of worship in the Free Churches.

The Ecumenical Movement, and, in particular, the Student Christian Movement as the interdenominational organization with a special responsibility for undergraduates, has fostered an ecclesiastical lend-lease

[1] R. H. Hutton, *Cardinal Newman* (1891), p. 196.

programme between the Anglican and Free Churches.
In general, the Anglicans may be said to have taught
the Free Churches the art of worship (though in the
spontaneity of free prayers and in hymns—their sung
creeds—the Free Churches had their own distinctive
contribution to make), while the Free Churches have
helped to teach Anglicans the art of preaching.[1] Moreover, the Bishop of Durham graciously acknowledges
that 'the works of Free Church scholars are widely read
and highly valued by Anglicans'.[2] Free Churchmen,
for their part, would gladly acknowledge their deep
indebtedness to such Anglican writers as Archbishop
William Temple and Sir Edwyn Hoskyns, Fr. Lionel
Thornton and Fr. A. G. Hebert, Dom Gregory Dix
and Canon Raven, amongst a host of others.

In many ways, other than liturgical or theological,
there has been a *rapprochement* between Anglicans and
Free Churchmen during the present century. The
causes are many: in part, it is due to the need to make
a Christian, as distinct from a party, stand against
secularism, where the cry must be 'Close the ranks';
in part to the recognition of the sin and folly of fissipar-
ousness in the mission-fields where these Churches are
co-operating (most notably in the Church of South
India); in part, to the friendship of Anglicans and Free
Churchmen in their undergraduate days at the ancient
and modern universities; and, most of all, it has been
the fruit of the Ecumenical Movement.

This interdenominational movement for reunion
derived its impetus from the great International

[1] cf. the present writer's *The Worship of the English
Puritans* (1948).
[2] *The Church of England*, by E. W. Watson, with Epilogue
by Alwyn Williams, p. 182.

Missionary Council meeting held at Edinburgh in 1910, and concluded the first phase of its development in the inauguration of the World Council of Churches at Amsterdam in 1948. The British organs of the Movement are the Conference of British Missionary Societies (1912), and the British Council of Churches (1942). The effect on English religious life has been twofold: these organizations have contributed to the formulation of a unified and orthodox theology (through the 'Faith and Order' Movement), and to a united policy in relation to the political and social implications of the Christian faith (through the 'Life and Work' Movement), as steps towards the realization of organic unity. Representative English Free Church leaders in the Ecumenical Movement have been: Sir Henry Lunn (Methodist), Dr. A. E. Garvie (Congregationalist), Henry T. Hodgkin (Quaker), and Dr. William Paton (Presbyterian).

While no organic unions have been consummated between unrelated churches in England,[1] marriages between related Communions have been arranged, notably that between the Wesleyan, United and Primitive Methodists in 1932. The most striking success was achieved overseas, when the Church of South India came into being, incorporating the former Anglican, Congregationalist, Methodist, and Presbyterian missionary churches in that vast area.

On the home field, however, a great degree of interdenominational co-operation has been achieved in the application of the Christian faith to the common life. Agreed syllabuses of religious instruction followed by agreed school service-books; joint deputations to the

[1] Nevertheless, important conversations with a view to reunion are proceeding between the Church of England and the Church of Scotland (Presbyterian), and between the Church of England and the Methodist Church.

Government at times of industrial, social, or international crisis; and combined operations in evangelism (such as the 'Religion and Life Weeks') are new phenomena in the religious life of the nation. The most notable of such joint actions was the publication of a declaration on the social implications of the Christian faith, which appeared, in the thick of the Second World War, over the signatures of the Archbishop of Canterbury, the Cardinal Archbishop of Westminster, the Moderator of the Church of Scotland, and the Moderator of the Free Church Federal Council. This fact alone would justify the claim of Dr. William Temple, in the sermon preached at his enthronement as Archbishop of Canterbury, that the Ecumenical Movement is 'the great new fact of our time'.

Moreover, the Free Churches have, in the Free Church Federal Council, an organ through which to define and present their common mind on the major issues of the day, as they affect their constituent bodies.

Those associations which Canon Roger Lloyd calls 'Handmaids of the Church' have also proved servants of the Free Churches.[1] The British and Foreign Bible Society continues to assist the common missionary expansion of the Churches by making available translations of the Scriptures in more than a thousand languages.[2] The Student Christian Movement, working amongst university students and the older pupils of schools, has trained many Free Church leaders, notable for their catholicity, and its allied organization, the Student Volunteer Movement, has sent a steady stream of missionary recruits to the ends of the earth.[3]

[1] *op. cit.*, 1, p. 178 f.
[2] See J. H. Ritson, *The World is our Parish* (1939).
[3] T. Tatlow, *The Story of the Student Christian Movement*, p. 299.

A further important interdenominational Christian organization is the Young Men's Christian Association (which celebrated the centenary of its foundation by Sir George Williams in 1944). With its sister organization, the Y.W.C.A., it has commended the Christian faith with considerable success to youth, and has taught the Churches to utilize modern techniques in reaching the churchless. Sometimes accused of being a substitute for the family life of the churches, it has nevertheless proved a valiant auxiliary in stemming the rising tide of materialism, and can be a most valuable liaison-officer between the churches and unevangelized youth, who would be suspicious often of a direct, ecclesiastical approach. All these handmaids, however, are part of the greater Movement for uniting the forces of Christendom against the encroachments of secularism and the omnicompetent modern State.

Contacts between the ministry and the churchless, which became increasingly tenuous in the early years of the century, were renewed by the children of the Free and other churches with great difficulty during the two World Wars. The chaplains became the champions of ecclesiastical unity, and of specialized ministries and new techniques of evangelism to bridge the gulf between the Church and the uncommitted. Specialized types of ministry have included industrial chaplaincies, Christian youth leaders, and the establishment of psychological and marriage-guidance clinics in association with some churches. The church youth-clubs performed such admirable services that the State copied their example.

New modes of evangelism were attempted with conspicuous success by the Methodists, and imitation proved to be the sincerest form of flattery. Already accustomed to vigorous and direct evangelism in their Central Halls, they were inspired by the example of Chadwick's Cliff College 'trekkers'. These Franciscan Methodists went out 'to preach the Gospel to the unreached everywhere, untrammelled by machinery, uninfluenced by schedules, and unhindered by entanglements'.[1] It seems that their evangelism on village greens, crowded race-courses, and packed pleasure-beaches, made an impression out of all proportion to their numbers. The same concern for the churchless multitudes was the foundation of the 'Christian Commando Campaigns' which sought to go to the people who would not go to church, and challenged them in factories, cinemas, and canteens. Another famous venture, 'Question Time' on Tower Hill, is associated with that excellent apologist, Dr. Donald Soper.

At the same time, several Free Church congregations, especially some in hostile territory, had been experimenting with religious drama and religious films as methods of evangelism. Some were discouraged by finding that those attending such services constituted an audience, not a worshipping congregation, and appreciated the sugar, but not the pill. Though success was local and limited, at first, in such ventures, techniques were to be improved out of all recognition. In the field of religious broadcasting, success, though more difficult to assess accurately, seems to have been more notable, and, if the uncommitted developed an 'armchair religion', that was better than none. In fact, the outstanding expositors presented the Christian faith and ethics challengingly to the sedentary. Moreover, the technique of broadcasting seems to have been largely responsible for the more concentrated brevity of the modern sermon,

[1] N. Dunning, *Samuel Chadwick* (1933), p. 234.

and the increasing preference for a confidential, intimate style of delivery, in place of rhetorical discourses.

The outstanding Free Church preachers of this century have been masters of distinctive pulpit styles. The expository style had its masters in Drs. Campbell Morgan and W. E. Sangster in Westminster and in Dr. J. D. Jones of Bournemouth. The devotional approach was best exemplified by Drs. J. H. Jowett and F. B. Meyer, as by the Rev. A. E. Whitham. Dr. Leslie D. Weatherhead was expert in the psychological approach at City Temple. The apologists of the pulpit included Professor H. H. Farmer and Dr. Donald Soper, and two impressive Cambridge laymen and historians, Dr. T. R. Glover and Mr. Bernard L. Manning. Even more remarkable than the presence of these giants was the improvement in the general level of Biblical scholarship as applied to the cultural context of the age of social, political, and economic revolution. Equally impressive was the reverent conduct of Divine worship and the celebration of the Sacraments in Free Churches. Congregations were smaller in the post-Christian age, but the quality of Christian understanding and commitment was greater.[1]

Perhaps the most obvious change amongst Free Churchmen has been the diminution of the cry for the disestablishment of the Church of England. In explanation, it might be stated that it is not due to any lessening of their conviction that the Church must be free of State entanglements to proclaim the Gospel, for their case has been confirmed by the example of contemporary Churches subjugated and muzzled by Nazi Ger-

---

[1] For a comparison of Anglican and Free Church preaching during the period see the present author's *Varieties of English Preaching: 1900–1960* (1963).

many and Soviet Russia; rather is it that they recognize both the State's need of religion and the benefits of State subsidies in the cases of chaplaincies in the hospitals and the Services, and of religious education in church schools. Moreover, both Anglican and Free Churches are inevitably missionary (and therefore 'gathered churches') in a largely indifferent England. Furthermore, neither tradition of churchmanship finds the State connexion a grievous handicap in its proclamation of the faith.

Another significant change in the life of the Free Churches has been the admission of women to the ranks of the ordained ministry in the Baptist and Congregational Churches. While few in number, they constitute an acknowledgement, perhaps long overdue, of the services rendered by women to the Church of God. The Methodists, under the inspiration of Hugh Price Hughes, have established a trained Order of Deaconesses.

Throughout the period the Free Churches have been served by scholars, preachers, and administrators of distinction. The Baptists have made a pre-eminent contribution to Old Testament studies, and the Methodists have also excelled in the same field. Congregationalists have distinguished themselves in biblical and systematic theology and in comparative religion. All four Churches are notably represented in the field of New Testament studies, as also in ecclesiastical history.

Perhaps the only two outstandingly creative theologians were Peter Taylor Forsyth, a Congregationalist, and John Oman, a Presbyterian. The former insisted in the Liberal wilderness on a return to distinctively Biblical categories and doctrines, enlivening his writing with pithy epigrams and piercing wit ('fireworks in a fog' was a description of his style); the latter produced in *The Natural and the Supernatural* a cogent and brilliant philosophical defence of the Christian faith. The Free Churches both in size and influence have outgrown, if they ever deserved, the designation of 'sects'. Ernst Troeltsch's distinction between 'church' and 'sect' types of religious organizations cannot be applied easily to the differences between the Church of England and the Free Churches of the twentieth century.[1] The Free Churches are no longer enclosed and private gardens within which the holy few may be separate, preserving their sanctity inviolate from the world's contamination. The English Free Churches are mother-churches of world communities to-day. The Baptists and the Methodists, to take two outstanding examples, have gathered vast harvests of souls in the Protestant world, each communion owning the allegiance of over twelve million members drawn from the five continents. Whilst the Presbyterian and Reformed Churches may claim an even larger in-gathering, Presbyterianism did not originate in England, but in Geneva; moreover, the present-day Presbyterian Church of England is historically in the main an offshoot of the Church of Scotland. None the less, it has had a missionary influence in India and China and Formosa, and has made a contribution to theological scholarship which is out of all proportion to its numbers. Congregationalism has a world-wide membership; though not comparable in size to either the Baptist or Methodist Churches, it has played a leading part in the theological and ecclesiastical life of the day, and is exceedingly influential in the U.S.A. The Society of Friends,

[1] E. Troeltsch, *The Social Teaching of the Christian Churches*, pp. 328 f., 697 f.

though technically not one of the Free Churches, has very close affinities with them, and its Christian humanitarianism has won approval in circles anti-ecclesiastical. It stands for a Christian pacifism, which is as courageous as it is practical in the organization of ambulance units and of relief work in war-shattered countries. All these ecclesiastical organizations, Presbyterianism alone excluded, are the products, under God, of English religious history. In their transatlantic expressions they are clearly destined to play an increasingly important role in the future.

Their basic principles of church-order will be their contribution to the One Holy Catholic Church Visible of the future: it is these which justify their continued existence. The chief of them is the conception of the Church as a 'gathered' community, consisting of those who have been called out of the world by Christ to minister in the world, and who have responded by a conscious dedication of their lives to the King and Head of the Church. Christians, the Free Churches claim, are not born; they are made by the Divine initiative and the human surrender in faith. They came into being as sects which protested against a Catholicity which had ceased to be Holy; they remain witnesses to holiness, but in their world-wide extent and missionary zeal they are developing the comprehensiveness of Catholicity. Founded upon a covenant-relationship between God and His people, which is an engagement of heart and will as well as of mind in the 'obedience of faith', they are utterly opposed to any merely nominal relationship to Christ and His Church.

In the second place, their forms of Church polity conserve the Crown Rights of Christ as Redeemer, and His exclusive right to rule in the churches, unfettered by the dictates of hierarchy or the favour of Caesar. They stand for Christocracy.

In the third place, they witness to the 'priesthood of all believers', and the apostolate of the laity. By this principle they declare positively that each church member is to be a missionary, and negatively they dissent from a double standard of Christian life (ascetic and non-ascetic) and sacerdotalism. Theirs is the true *via media* between an Ultramontanism which claims too much power for the Church, and an Erastianism which claims too much for the State. Their assertion of the priesthood of all believers is the secret of their contribution to democracy, by transference from the spiritual to the political sphere, and of their success in evangelism by the utilization of lay-preachers. This principle also explains their close contact with the common people in the hey-day of their history, in promoting their rights during the Commonwealth period, the Chartist Riots, and the foundation of the Independent Labour Party.

In the fourth place, their recognition of the primacy of the Gospel over the Church, of revelation over its institutional expressions, has given them an elasticity and flexibility rarely evidenced in Catholic structures of Church organization. In large measure it has also provided them with that precious heritage of freedom, limited only by their loyalty to Christ the King and Head of the Church.

Like every other Communion or group of Communions, they are fragments of the *Una Sancta*, and therefore incomplete. They pray for the fulfilment of our Lord's High-priestly Prayer *ut omnes unum sint*, believing that they have treasures to receive as well as to give, forgiveness to beg and to grant, in the One Holy Catholic and Apostolic Church *Visible* that is to be.

SELECT BIBLIOGRAPHY

THE following bibliography is merely a selection of the vast literature on the subject. It consists only of those volumes which are accessible and might interest the general reader. Books are listed only once, but they may be relevant to other chapters.

GENERAL

H. DAVIES, *The Worship of the English Puritans* (1948).

B. L. MANNING, *Essays in Orthodox Dissent* (1938).

— *The Making of Modern English Religion* (1929).

N. MICKLEM (Ed.), *A Book of Personal Religion* (1938).

E. A. PAYNE, *The Free Church Tradition in the Life of England* (1944).

F. M. POWICKE, *The Reformation in England* (1941).

CHAPTER I. PURITANS AND PREDECESSORS

W. H. FRERE and DOUGLAS (Eds.), *Puritan Manifestoes* (2nd edn. N. Sykes, 1954).

W. HALLER, *The Rise of Puritanism* (1938, 1957 paperback).

R. HOOKER, *Of the Laws of Ecclesiastical Politie* (Bk. V, 1957). (Also 'Everyman' edn.)

LUCY HUTCHINSON, *Memoirs of Colonel Hutchinson* (edn. of 1908).

M. M. KNAPPEN, *Tudor Puritanism* (1939).

G. F. NUTTALL, *The Holy Spirit in Puritan Faith and Experience* (1946).

P. A. SCHOLES, *The Puritans and Music* (1934).

A. S. P. WOODHOUSE, *Puritanism and Liberty* (1938).

CHAPTER II. CONFORMING AND NON-CONFORMING PURITANS

C. BURRAGE, *The Early English Dissenters in the Light of Recent Research* (2 vols., 1912).

L. H. CARLSON (Ed.), *The Writings of Henry Barrow, 1587–1590* (1962).

— *The Writings of John Greenwood, 1587–1590* (1962).

A. PEEL, *The First Congregational Churches* (1920).

A. PEEL (Ed.), *The Notebook of John Perry*, 1593 (1944).

A. PEEL and L. H. CARLSON (Eds.), *Cartwrightiana* (1951).

A. PEEL and L. H. CARLSON (Eds.), *The Writings of Robert Harrison and Robert Browne* (1953).

A. SIMPSON, *Puritanism in England and New England* (1955).

CHAPTER III. PRESBYTERIANS, CONGREGATIONALISTS, AND BAPTISTS

W. BRADFORD, *History of Plimouth Plantation* (edn. of 1900, Boston).

J. MOFFATT, *The Presbyterian Churches* (1928).

H. W. ROBINSON, *The Faith and Life of the Baptists* (1928).

A. C. UNDERWOOD, *A History of the English Baptists* (1947).

CHAPTER IV. UNDER THE COMMONWEALTH AND PROTECTORATE

T. CARLYLE, *Oliver Cromwell's Letters and Speeches* (Collected Works, vols. 14–18, 1869).

F. E. HUTCHINSON, *Milton and the English Mind* (1946).

R. M. JONES, *The Faith and Practice of the Quakers* (1927).

J. M. LLOYD-THOMAS (Ed.), *The Autobiography of Richard Baxter* (1931).

JOHN MILTON, *Apology for Smectymnuus* and *Of Reformation in England* ('Everyman' edn. of 1927).

G. F. NUTTALL, *Visible Saints, The Congregational Way, 1640–1660* (1957).

R. S. PAUL, *The Lord Protector* (1955).

L. F. SOLT, *Saints in Arms* (1959).

CHAPTER V. UNDER THE CROSS OF PERSECUTION

W. C. BRAITHWAITE, *The Beginnings of Quakerism* (2nd ed., 1955).

JOHN BUNYAN, *Pilgrim's Progress.*
— *Grace Abounding to the Chief of Sinners.*
G. N. CLARK, *The Later Stuarts* (1934).
G. R. CRAGG, *Puritanism in the period of the Great Persecution* (1957).
JOHN EVELYN, *Diary* (edn. of 1907).
C. H. FIRTH, *Essays Historical and Literary* (1938).
GEORGE FOX, *Journal* (ed. N. Penney, 1924).
A. PEEL (Ed.), *Essays Congregational and Catholic* (1931).
SAMUEL PEPYS, *Diary* (ed. Braybrooke, 1825).
F. J. POWICKE, *Life of the Reverend Richard Baxter* (2 vols., 1924, 1927).
— *The Cambridge Platonists* (1926).
J. W. ASHLEY SMITH, *The Birth of Modern Education; the contribution of the Dissenting Academies, 1660–1800* (1954).

CHAPTER VI. THE AGE OF TOLERATION

A. D. BELDEN, *George Whitefield the Awakener* (n.d.).
H. BETT, *The Spirit of Methodism* (1937).
G. R. CRAGG, *From Puritanism to the Age of Reason* (1950).
D. COOMER, *English Dissent* (1947).
H. DAVIES, *Worship and Theology in England, From Watts and Wesley to Maurice, 1690–1850* (1961).
A. P. DAVIS, *Isaac Watts* (1943).
B. L. MANNING, *The Hymns of Wesley and Watts* (1942).
G. F. NUTTALL (Ed.), *Philip Doddridge, 1702–1751* (1951).
N. SYKES, *Church and State in England in the Eighteenth Century* (1934).
JOHN WESLEY, *Journal* (8 vols., Ed., N. Curnock, 1938).
J. H. WHITELEY, *Wesley's England* (1938).

CHAPTER VII. THE ERA OF EXPANSION

R. COWHERD, *The Politics of English Dissent . . . 1815–1848* (1956).
A. W. W. DALE, *Life of R. W. Dale of Birmingham* (1899).
H. DAVIES, *Worship and Theology in England, From Newman to Martineau, 1850–1900* (1962).

M. Edwards, *Methodism and England* (1943).
R. C. K. Ensor, *England, 1870–1914* (1936).
É. Halévy, *A History of the English People* (3 vols., 1924).
J. L. and B. Hammond, *The Bleak Age* (1934).
D. P. Hughes, *The Life of Hugh Price Hughes by his Daughter* (1904).
K. S. Latourette, *A History of the Expansion of Christianity* (vol. IV, 1947).
J. E. Orr, *The Second Evangelical Awakening in Britain* (1944).
A. Peel, *These Hundred Years, 1831–1931* (1931). (Congregationalism.)
J. E. Rattenbury, *Wesley's Legacy to the World* (1928).
R. F. Wearmouth, *Methodism and the Working-Class Movements of England* (1937).

CHAPTER VIII.   THE TWENTIETH CENTURY

F. Baker, *A Charge to Keep* (1947). (Methodism.)
S. W. Carruthers, *Fifty Years: 1876–1926.* (Presbyterianism.)
D. R. Davies, *On to Orthodoxy* (1939).
H. Davies, *Varieties of English Preaching: 1900–1960* (1963).
N. Dunning, *Samuel Chadwick* (1933).
P. T. Forsyth, *The Work of Christ* (1910, reprinted with a Memoir in 1938).
R. Lloyd, *The Church of England in the Twentieth Century* (Vol. I, 1946; II, 1950).
J. Marchant, *Dr. John Clifford, C.H.* (1924).
J. A. R. Marriott and A. Peel, *Robert Forman Horton* (1937).
W. E. Orchard, *From Faith to Faith* (1933).
G. S. Spinks, *Religion in Britain Since 1900* (1952).
T. Tatlow, *The Story of the Student Christian Movement of Great Britain and Ireland* (1933).
E. W. Watson and Alwyn Williams, *The Church of England* (third edn., 1961).

INDEX

Academies, 11, 96, 103–7
Academy, Gale's, 106; Morton's, 105; Newport Pagnell, 143; Northampton, 107; Tewkesbury, 106
Act of Supremacy, 21
— of Toleration, 103, 119
— of Uniformity (1559), 21, 22; (1662), 13, 93–8, 100, 104, 117
— to Retain the Queen's Majesty's Servants in due Obedience, 48
Admonition, First, 30–1; *Second,* 30, 43; *to Parliament,* 43
Advertisements, 29
Anabaptists, 33, 34, 58, 59, 70, 84
Arminians, 60: as General Baptists, 61, 71

Baptist Theological Colleges, 154
Baptists, 1, 8, 9, **33–6,** 41, 49, 50, 51, **58–62,** 70, 71–2, 89, 90, 143, 161, 180, 197–8; Calvinistic, 61; first English Congregation of, 55; General, 61, 71–3; growth of, 175; in economic life, 103; missionary movement of, 141; Particular, 61, 71; service books of, 189; under Charles II, 91–4; women in ministry of, 197
Barrowe, 31, 48, 51, 53

Barrowists, 31–2
Baxter, Richard, 13, 64, **78–81,** 83, 89, 92, 96, 97, 101
Bell, Andrew, 149
Bible Christians, 177
—, Protestant conception of the authority of, 3–4, **18–19,** 24, 28, 43, 68
Biblical criticism, 178–81
Black Rubric, 15, 47
Book of Common Prayer, 15–17, 21, 23–5, 44, 47, 92–5, 146
Booth, William, 177
Brewster, William, 54
Browne, Robert, 32, 33, 48, **51–3**
Brownists, **32–3**
Bucer, Martin, 15
Bunting, Jabez, 156–7
Bunyan, John, 101, **111–13**
Burial Laws, 147

Calvin, John, 13, 14, 15
Carey, William, 172, 173
Cartwright, Thomas, 10, 19, 27, 30, **41–3,** 46, 48
Catholic Apostolic Church sect, 177
Channel Islands, 41, 46–7
Charles I, 24, 63–5, 103
— II, 91–2, 112
Clarendon Code, 9, 85, 92–104, 105, 117; repeal of, 145
Congregational service books, 189
Congregationalists, 1, 37–8, 41, 49, **50–8,** 60, 122, 141, 143, 161–2, 180,

DATE DUE

HIGHSMITH 45-220